STANLEYBEAMAN&SEARS
TWENTY FIVE YEARS

VISUAL PROFILE BOOKS, NEW YORK

Principals from left to right: Don Glitzsis, Veronique Pryor, Portia Ellis, Betsy Beaman, Kimberly Stanley, and Burn Sears

PREFACE

The principals of Stanley Beaman & Sears have a shared vision that has developed over the course of a 30 - year friendship and professional association. With a collaborative working style and an appetite for innovation, they started the firm to focus on unique or pioneering projects in healthcare, higher education and the arts -- building types that, in their view, represented "civilization's great institutions".
Stanley Beaman & Sears is unique in that the principals work collaboratively with their staff on each project from start to finish, focusing on function, form and technical issues respectively. Their level of personal involvement is unique in the industry.
Accordingly, Stanley Beaman & Sears has attracted a "family of creative thinkers" to collaborate in the design and execution of these special projects, focusing on a handful of select clients whose projects receive the firm's best ideas and undivided attention. Often characterized as a "big idea" firm, their strength lies in their ability to forge creative partnerships, and collaborate with clients in the exploration and achievement of their facility goals.

The creative talent that makes up the professional staff includes a diverse group of architects, interior designers and graphic designers, many who have additional degrees in Business, Fine Arts, Mathematics, Physics or Information Technology. Their collective experience, versatility and technical depth has consistently resulted in innovative and award-winning projects. The work of Stanley Beaman & Sears has been featured in such diverse publications as Architectural Record, Contract Design Magazine, Modern Healthcare and The Wall Street Journal.

Since its inception, the firm has worked on projects ranging from $2 million to $240 million in construction cost ~ from innovative health and university facilities to projects for the arts. Their strength lies in their ability to forge creative partnerships, and collaborate with clients in the exploration and achievement of their facility goals.

A FAMILY OF CREATIVE THINKERS

Three is a powerful number in mathematics, science, religion and countless other human endeavors. That may not have been a consideration when three young Atlanta architects, Kimberly Stanley, AIA, Betsy Beaman, AIA, IIDA, SEGD, and Burn Sears, AIA, turned their mutual interest in collaborative work and their shared appetite for innovation into an architecture practice in 1992. The award-winning firm they founded has managed to create one life-changing, technically advanced and beautifully crafted facility after another for clients in healthcare, pediatrics, higher education, research and the arts in the 25 years since its founding. To make a positive difference in the world through such challenging building types is certainly powerful in ways that would gratify any three architects.

The trio immediately set the bar high by focusing on building types that, in their view, housed "civilization's great institutions." In fact, each individual's skills, experiences and passions have extended well beyond achieving excellence in design. Not only has Stanley focused on designing facilities for healthcare and higher education, she promotes children's health and education through advocacy and fundraising. Beaman uses her passion for art and design to win design awards, act as lecturer and critic at colleges and universities, and serve such arts organizations as the Zuckerman Museum of Art and Arts Leaders of Metro Atlanta. For Sears, his enthusiasm for producing innovative architectural solutions is matched by his commitment to project management, building technology and construction methodology—along with strict adherence to budget and scheduling parameters.

As they built a successful firm that currently numbers some 50 employees, Stanley, Beaman and Sears established a unique way of working among their "family of creative thinkers" that is open, collaborative and multi-disciplinary. The principals have worked collaboratively with staff members on each project from day one, focusing on function, form and technical issues respectively, at a level of personal involvement that is unique in the profession. Directing what is often characterized as a "big idea" firm, they draw additional strength from their ability to forge creative partnerships with clients in the exploration and achievement of their facility goals. In fact, their willingness to blend the collective experience, versatility and technical depth of clients and staff members has consistently resulted in innovative and award-winning projects.

Where ideas come from

To spend a typical day at Stanley Beaman & Sears is to be immersed in an open, diverse and collegial studio environment where the world of ideas is taken seriously and everyone is a potential student, ready to listen and learn as well as to explore and create. Staff members—many with additional degrees in business, fine arts, mathematics, physics or information technology—are chosen for their talent, ambition and motivation, sustaining a culture of innovation at the firm. Everyone respects the basic values of design, engineering, construction and technology. Yet art has its place in the studio as well. The firm maintains Gallery 180, an in-house art gallery that seeks to nurture the connection between the fine arts and architecture, to bring contemporary artists and their work to the office, guaranteeing that art represents more virtual reality to the staff.

Because good ideas tend to cross traditional boundaries, the firm functions as an integrated design practice, where the lines between architecture, interior design and environmental graphic design are blurred and everyone works to blend these disciplines seamlessly into a continuous design process. Project teams are filled with members from each design discipline to ensure that the overall design presents a unified vision. To ensure maximum communication and collaboration, everyone works side by side in project studios, in sharp contrast with firms that organize their design disciplines as distinct entities and even house them in non-contiguous work environments. Each person on a project team at Stanley Beaman & Sears can contribute to the design as it evolves, providing the cross-pollination and exchange of ideas that lead to stronger solutions and dynamic building programs.

It's exhilarating to observe what this organizational culture can produce, especially when knowledgeable clients join the discussion. The firm takes the responsibility of bringing a building into the world very seriously. With careful consideration of all the forces acting on a new project environment, ranging from architecture, engineering and design factors to geographic, economic and social conditions, a project team can create a design that respectfully and organically connects a space to its permanent occupants, visiting public, immediate site and surrounding community. The resulting addition to the built environment shapes the world it enters and is shaped by it in turn, demonstrating the power of place.

How the future will look

Focusing on the design of facilities for healthcare, pediatrics, higher education, research and the arts means taking aim at a moving target. The restless evolution of these institutions is ideal for Stanley Beaman & Sears. Besides satisfying the firm's desire for innovation, they encourage it to push the boundaries of possibility, explore new technologies, and work harder to reveal the strengths of every project. Changing conditions for the science, practice and economics of healthcare, for example, ensure that no architect or interior designer in the field can succeed by resting on past laurels. Stanley Beaman & Sears knows its buildings will remain at the forefront of contemporary design only if its people are willing to keep questioning how design can better serve its constituents.

When asked what the future holds for the firm, the partners look forward to more challenging commissions in healthcare and education, greater diversity in the types of clients being served, new opportunities for the interior design and environmental graphic design studios, and projects that allow the firm to explore design at a larger scale. So the future could bring new design, technical and professional accomplishments that break precedents and launch new traditions in the office and beyond.

Whatever the future holds, Stanley Beaman & Sears firmly declares that it is passionate about design. In a world that ceaselessly shifts and redefines itself, the firm stands ready to help stage those spaces that society needs to thrive. As it sincerely declares: "We live and work in buildings. We spend hours between walls and under a roof. We believe that our surroundings play an important role in the way we think about and interact with the world. Our goal is to create powerful places that demonstrate our respect for the community, culture and resources invested in extraordinary architecture."

CONTENTS

1990'S Representative Projects

2000'S Representative Projects

2010'S Representative Projects

Conceptual Projects

LAWRENCEVILLE SENIOR CENTER
Lawrenceville, Georgia

Whether or not Baby Boomers can redefine aging on their own, relentlessly upbeat terms, they will find encouragement and fellowship at facilities like Lawrenceville Senior Center, in Lawrenceville, Georgia. Designed by Stanley Beaman & Sears for Gwinnett County, the one-story, 12,500-square-foot contemporary facility is located in 162-acre Rhodes Jordan Park on the edge of a large reservoir lake, making it convenient and appealing to County residents. The architecture responds to its idyllic surroundings with two ship-like forms, a larger structure sheathed in glass and preformed metal shingles, reminiscent of fish scales, that looks poised to sail and a smaller one enclosed in split-faced concrete that remains moored to the land.

Interestingly, the Center's interior reflects the early involvement of senior citizens whose insights shaped the project's conceptual phase. Underscoring the fact that learning, activity, ingenuity and curiosity are not the exclusive realm of youth, the accommodations include a multi-purpose room for exercise and dance classes, a dining area, dedicated rooms for billiards, arts and crafts, table games and other popular activities, and ADA-accessible restrooms. Appreciated for its planned activities, scheduled events such as talks about medical, financial, and consumer issues, and hot lunches served every weekday, the Center has quickly become popular among Gwinnett County residents 60 and older.

As Charlotte Nash, Gwinnett County Board of Commissioners Chairwoman, noted at the ribbon-cutting, the new facility arrived not a moment too soon. "Seniors now make up more than 13 percent of the Gwinnett population," Nash observed, "and we must continue planning for this expected growth."

Building Exterior

A. Lakeside view

B. Plan / elevation

C. Dining porch

D. Computer renderings

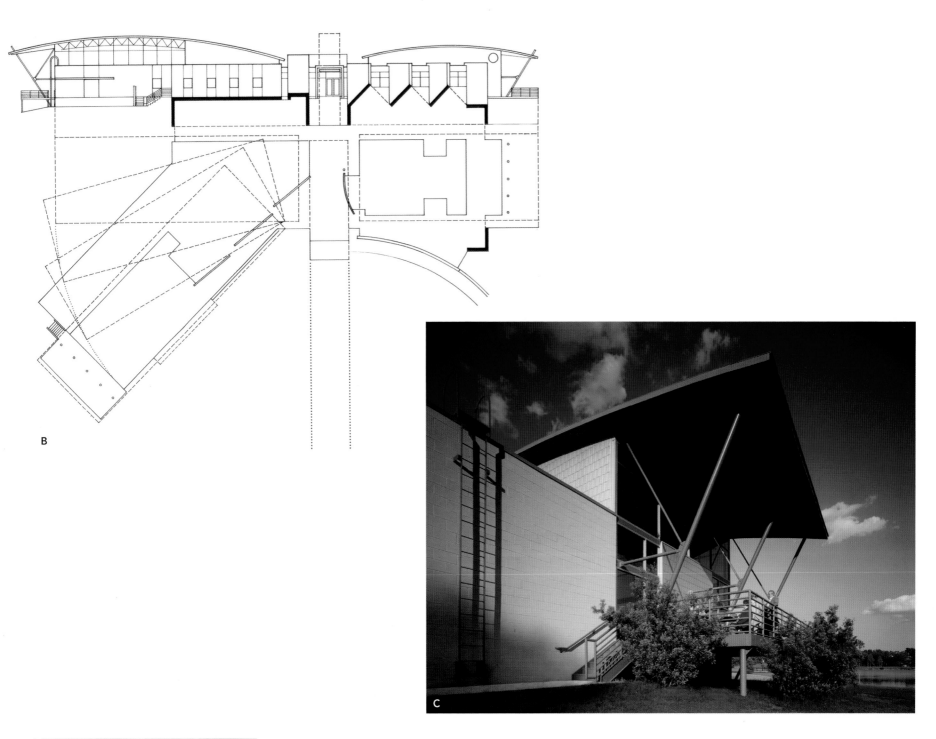

B

C

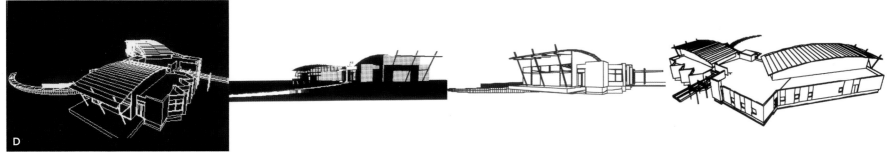

D

A. Exterior dining hall
B. Ramp to lake
C. Interior dining hall
D. Waiting area

H.J.C. BOWDEN SENIOR MULTIPURPOSE CENTER
East Point, Georgia

With one out of five citizens in metropolitan Atlanta projected to be over age 60 by 2030, the 1995 inauguration of the H.J.C. Bowden Senior Multipurpose Center, in East Point, a suburb in Fulton County southwest of Atlanta, has proved to be a popular source of health, social, nutritional and educational activities for seniors. The one-story, 25,000-square foot structure was designed by Stanley Beaman & Sears for Fulton County to house such diverse activities as a fitness center, heated pool, adult day care, computer laboratory, medical clinic, dining hall, library, game room and varied pursuits like arts and crafts, self-help, support groups and social clubs.

The first facility of its kind in Fulton County, Bowden has put a modern face on aging. There is certainly nothing outdated about its bold design and animated forms, from the perfectly machined architecture of glass, metal and brick to the sunny and spacious interior of wood, concrete and natural slate flooring. Bowden advertises its accessibility through multiple "front doors" to its offerings. With the façades of its main pavilion and two wings almost completely transparent, it not only connects occupants with the world, it welcomes the community inside.

What grounds the building in its time are such details as the handcrafted stone wall that runs through the entire space, contrasting with the precision of metal, glass and brick, the elliptical "spa" of reinforced concrete, enclosing the heated pool in a womb-like envelope, and the comfortable accommodations, where seniors are enthusiastically redefining what it means to grow old.

Canopy at main entry

A. Dining hall

B. Main reception

C. Pivot doors at dining hall

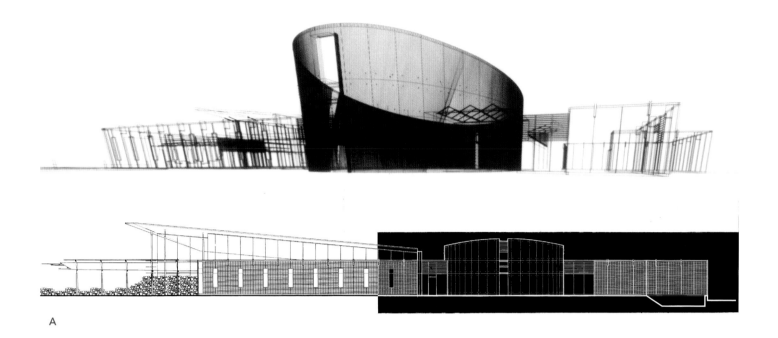

A

B

A. Computer renderings

B. Skylight over heated pool

C. Pre-function area

Twilight view of entry and activity rooms

AUGUSTA UNIVERSITY HEALTH
CHILDREN'S HOSPITAL OF GEORGIA

Augusta, Georgia

How should the next generation of children's healthcare facilities function? Responding to this challenge, the 154-bed, five-story, 220,000-square-foot Children's Hospital of Georgia, designed by Stanley Beaman & Sears and located in Augusta's Midtown neighborhood with floor-by-floor connections to Augusta University Medical Center, was planned around the philosophy of "family-centered care." To support this philosophy, the only institution in its region dedicated exclusively to children refocused its planning from perpetuating the existing system to viewing its operations as families would experience them, simultaneously encouraging families to participate in the process.

The design resulted in a modern facility that is also a pioneer in treating children. Not only has Children's Hospital dispelled old notions about hospitals, it has enriched the healing environment with educational and entertainment capabilities. Its award-winning design provides such essential facilities as a pediatric emergency department, six-OR surgical suite, radiology and imaging, Level I PICU, Level IV NICU, single- and double-occupancy patient rooms, and laboratories, along with such amenities as a lobby, welcome center, admissions, dining room, gift shop, chapel, conference center and parking.

Yet its embrace of a "nature and technology" theme and its inclusion of family-friendly spaces greatly expand its mission. Thus, visitors find an Archeological Dig Playscape, Video Aquarium and Technological Arbor at the entrance, mostly private patient rooms, family lounges with kitchenettes and sleep rooms, schoolroom and teachers office, family resource center, financial counseling, playrooms, family laundry and family rooftop garden. Children's Hospital is optimistic, helpful and assuring, qualities every child and parent can appreciate.

Main entrance

A

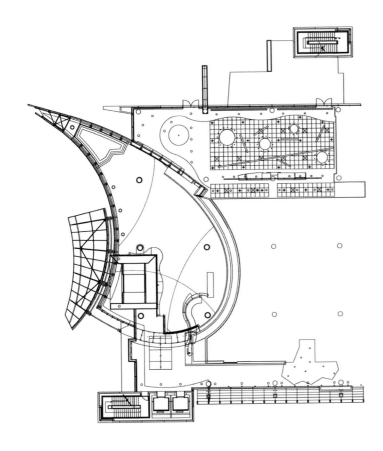

B

C

D

A. Detail main entry facade

B. Main lobby floor plan

C. Detail composition

D. View of main entry and curved glass facade

Detail of surgery waiting

Arbor columns and computer circuit board pattern on glass facade

A. Main lobby

B. Video totems

C. Twilight view of exterior

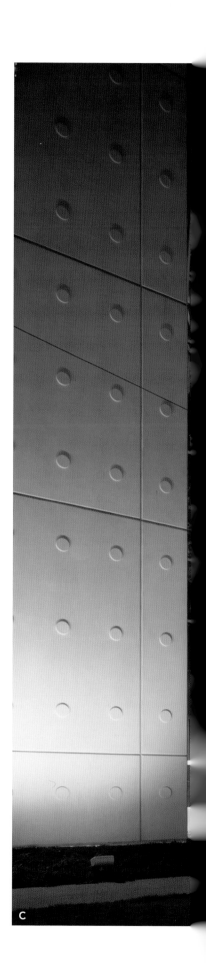

NORTH OAKS MEDICAL CENTER
Hammond, Louisiana

Hammond is a city of some 20,000 residents in Tangipahoa Parish, Louisiana, whose strategic location between Baton Rouge and New Orleans makes it an important center for highway-rail-air-sea transportation and distribution. But it is also a distressed community, where the median household income is $24,067 (2010 Census) and declining health statistics and lagging educational scores complicate everyday life. An ambitious and creatively conceived renovation and expansion of North Oaks Medical Center, designed by Stanley Beaman & Sears, has given the 330-bed general hospital in Hammond--one of Louisiana's largest and most progressive community hospitals--the means to improve the region's wellbeing.

Recognizing the relationship between education and wellness, North Oaks adopted a multi-disciplinary approach to enhancing community health, not just increasing outpatient services, but also bringing community education to its 60-acre campus. A new Medical Office and Administrative Building, upgraded Central Plant and site infrastructure, and new, five-story, 400,000-square-foot "Signature Building," which includes extensive educational facilities along with new emergency services, radiology, cardiology, inpatient bed floors, outpatient surgery and support services, have given North Oaks a reinvigorated self-image. It boldly challenges a status quo equating "hospital" with "illness."

From its generous, resort-like landscaping and cool, hotel-like architecture to its open, sun-drenched and attractive contemporary interior, North Oaks makes patients feel assured and their families feel welcome. Nearly 100 percent of patient beds, for example, have private rooms, where a calm, healing environment lets family members participate in care giving. With progressive facilities like these, the future of Hammond's residents looks considerably brighter.

Entry canopy amd drop-off

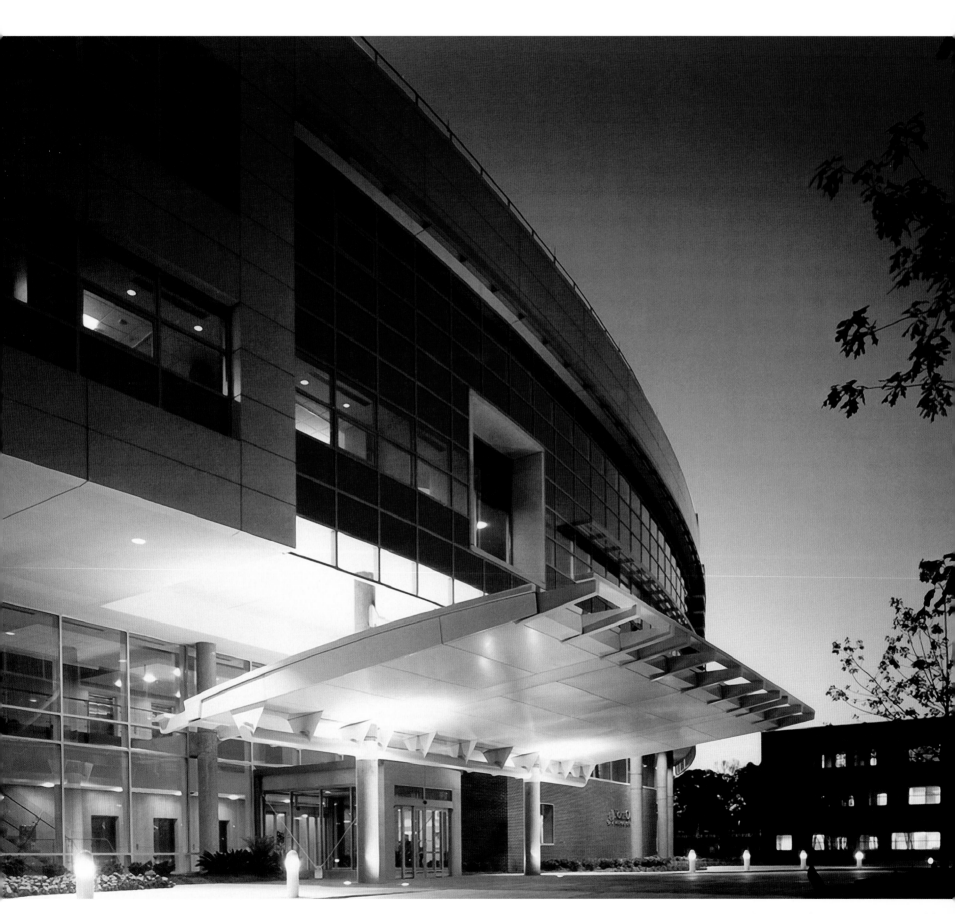

A. Two story lobby

B. Typical patient unit

C. Emergency department

D. Exterior detail

A

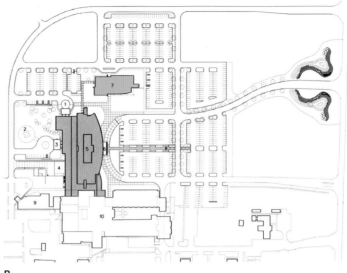

A. Twilight view of exterior

B. Site plan

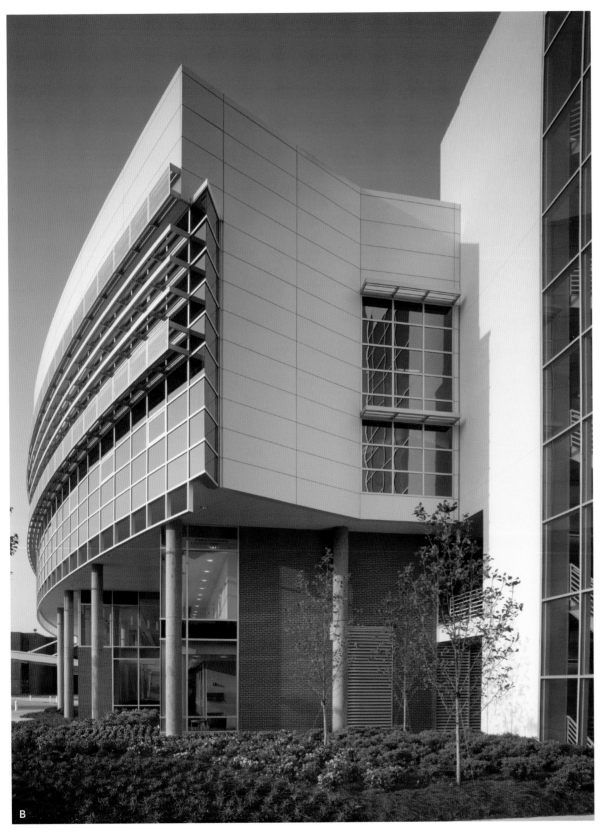

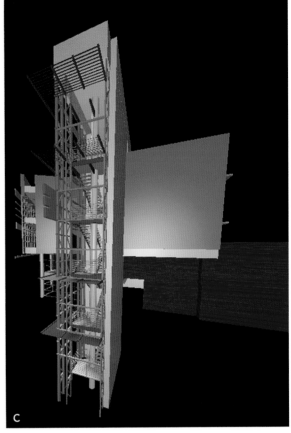

A. Medical office and administrative building

B. Detail of curved facade

C. Stair rendering

INTERACTIVE PLANET
Atlanta, Georgia

Many distinguished American businesses began in their founders' garages, including Walt Disney, Hewlett Packard, Nike and Apple. Yet a professionally designed workplace becomes a necessity at some point as an enterprise develops into a complex, organized and thriving organization. For Interactive Planet, a vanguard Web development company, that moment occurred when its leaders realized that having a formal office environment--one that would be imaginative, comfortable and conducive to collaborative engagement--could improve business efficiency and enhance recruitment. To accomplish this, the company commissioned Stanley Beaman & Sears to design a two-floor, 8,000-square-foot office in downtown Atlanta that would provide open workstations, video projection theater, video conference room, fitness room, and private offices for managers, Web designer and video/sound production staff.

It was fitting that Interactive Planet sought a radical and pioneering image for its space, since the project required the complete interior demolition and redesign of an existing building. What the design team conceived was a unique, open-plan circular studio, shaped by curving and angular forms that resemble an intergalactic panorama. The construction, accordingly, incorporates innovative design concepts and materials.

For example, the back-illuminated, sloped display wall that hovers over the space like a NASA satellite tracking screen, is constructed of wood and steel clad in Lexan® plastic sheeting, perforated metal panels and stainless steel checkered tread plate. Custom theatrical lighting illuminates the windowless design studio to an appropriate level without creating glare on computer monitors. Mobile workstations encourage informal meetings and interaction. Welcome to 21st-century commerce.

Web design studio

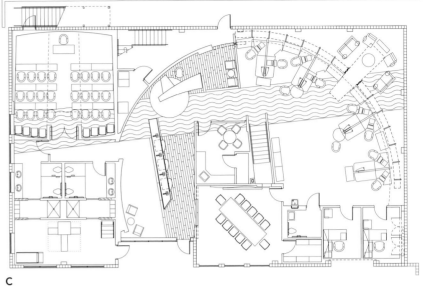

C

B

A. View from second floor

B. Main reception

C. Floor plan

Main reception desk

Detail of stairs

Typical workstation

UNIVERSITY OF NORTH GEORGIA
HEALTH AND NATURAL SCIENCE CENTER
Dahlonega, Georgia

On a hilltop site overlooking the 120-acre campus of the University of North Georgia in Dahlonega, the Health and Natural Science Building can be regarded as a beacon of enlightenment embodying ideas about education in general and the natural sciences in particular. One reason why this four-story, 120,000-square-foot building, designed by Stanley Beaman & Sears, enjoys such prominence is obviously its elevated site. Another reason is that the angular, crystalline contemporary structure--which reprise the irregular geometry of minerals mined along with gold and semi-precious gems in the region's mountains--contrasts with its architecturally traditional campus. A third reason is that the design is very responsive to the needs of its occupants, including the Departments of Nursing, Physical Therapy and Biology.

The architecture is dramatic, to be sure. In the lobby, the curtain wall recalls the geometry of minerals, a thrusting, slanted form anchors the space like a mine's shaft house, and the stair leading uphill to the building's main entry suggests a slice into the earth. Within the main building, a ramp continues this ascent, within the "mineshaft," to the building's upper floors, symbolizing the ongoing journey through life toward knowledge.
But the interior is as pragmatic as it is striking. From the main lobby, the building splits into two wings. One serves the functional needs of the three university departments with classrooms, laboratories, offices and a small, primary care clinic, while the other addresses the larger public, offering a 350-seat art lecture hall flanked by a media center, including a health science library, computer laboratories and 50-seat planetarium.

As the initial phase in a campus expansion master plan, the Health and Natural Science Building opens a new and promising chapter for the University, a school formed in 2013 by the consolidation of North Georgia College & State University, founded in 1873 in Dahlonega, and Gainesville State College, founded in 1964 in Gainesville.

Main entry

B

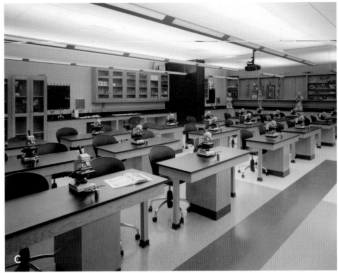

C

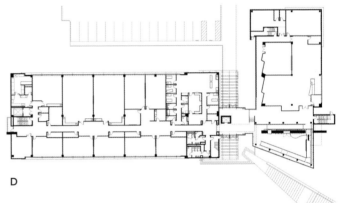

D

A. Approach towards main entry

B. Lobby and exhibit wall

C. Biology lab

D. First floor plan

A. View of lobby from upper floor

B. Detail of clerestory

C. Longitudinal view through lobby and classroom wing

A. Detail of castellated curtainwall supports

B. Lobby and ramp details

EMORY UNIVERSITY
WINSHIP CANCER INSTITUTE
Atlanta, Georgia

Documenting a history of cancer care, research and medical training dating back to the opening of its Robert Winship Clinic in 1937, Atlanta's Emory University was strongly motivated to develop the new Winship Cancer Institute. Indeed, the seven-story, 260,000-square-foot clinical and research facility, designed by Stanley Beaman & Sears, has been designated by the National Cancer Institute as Georgia's first and only Cancer Center, ensuring patients access to clinical trials and resources available only at designated Cancer Centers. The building gracefully commands a restrictive site within Emory's dense medical complex.

Outside, Winship acknowledges the Emory campus's Italianate-style architecture with a contemporary interpretation centered on a monumental, illuminated stair tower. Inside, its clean, modern setting, with the lower four levels dedicated to clinical care and upper three levels holding research laboratories, celebrates biological research and articulates a language of endeavor and affirmation. Patients and their families enter via the main lobby and proceed to such destinations as examination rooms, radiation oncology and imaging department, state-of-the-art linear accelerators, ambulatory infusion center, bone marrow transplant/hematology and leukemia clinic, and women's center. Research floors, by contrast, provide flexible, open plan laboratories and offices in configurations that encourage scientists to socialize and share information.

Pragmatic as Winship undoubtedly is, it also accommodates such family-friendly amenities as a family resource center, chapel, financial counseling and café. The interior is also rich in symbolism. Within the iconic stair tower, for example, transparent glass parapets enhance its openness, while inspirational words embedded into the landings--"caring," "courage" and "hope" on the clinical floors, and "imagination," "discovery" and "translation" on the laboratory floors—stimulate conversation and make social encounters easy and inviting. Custom light fixtures in the main lobby are reminiscent of microscope slides, and whiteboards along the corridors of research floors are lightly etched with the genetic codes of a flower, a butterfly and human being. An image of the double helix, a Winship logo, is also embedded in the terrazzo flooring in several places. At every turn patients, clinicians and researchers are reassured that they have come together in a single building to pursue a vital, storied mission.

Main entry

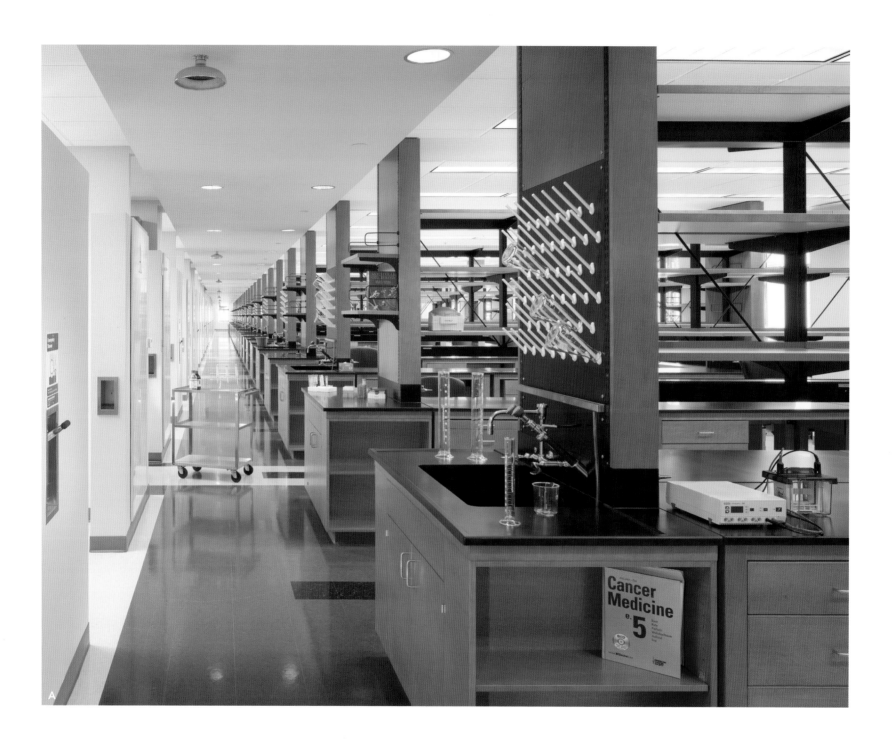

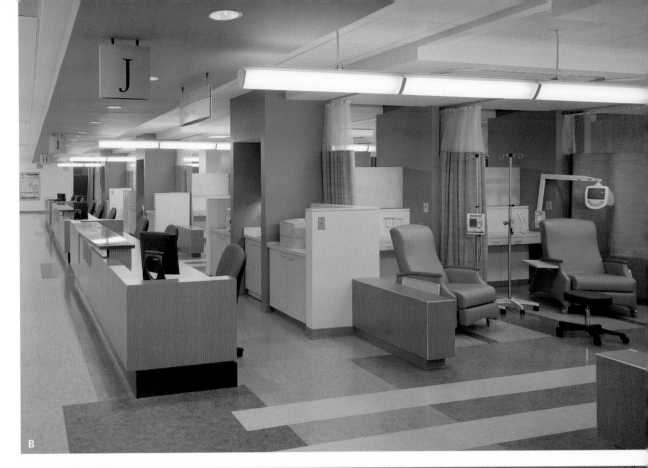

A. Research lab

B. Infusion center

C. Research floor

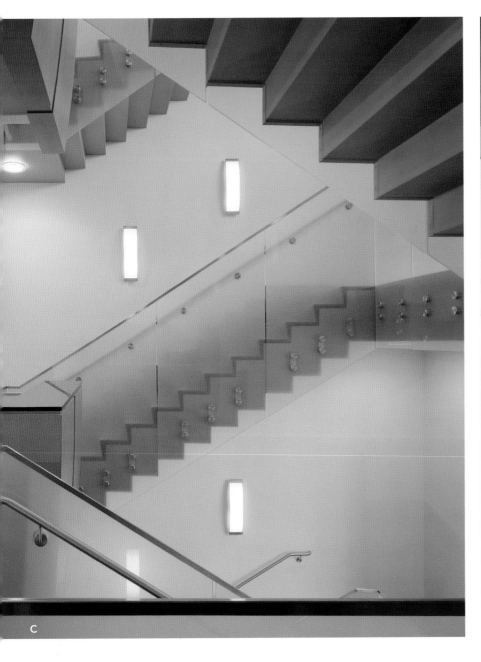

A. Transitional stair between clinics and research floor

B. Details

C. Stair details

D. Stair details

RADIOLOGY ASSOCIATES OF TALLAHASSEE
Tallahassee, Florida

Imaging is stressful for any patient, whether the patient requires diagnostic or interventional radiology. Aside from the individual's medical concerns, there are also physical and emotional inconveniences imposed by the facilities and equipment. For this reason, Radiology Associates of Tallahassee, a partnership of 17 board-certified radiologists, commissioned Stanley Beaman & Sears to design a new, three-story, 58,000-square-foot imaging center to create a calm and reassuring atmosphere for patients in addition to consolidating its offices and expanding its capabilities.

The facility accomplishes this with unmistakable confidence, welcoming patients to an environment of openness and caring expressed by a contemporary architecture of orthogonal and curving forms in glass, metal and brick. The interior design de-mystifies and softens its high-tech environment with a hospitality-style atmosphere more suggestive of a hotel or spa than a medical facility. Once patients leave the soaring, two-story entry lobby with its curving glass wall, they encounter such thoughtful accommodations as separate sub-waiting rooms for male and female patients, imaging suites projecting peace and tranquility, treatment rooms not shared with medical equipment, a Women's Imaging Center, and interiors appointed in soothing earth tones, natural finishes, comfortable furnishings and artwork. In addition, administrative functions and staff amenities are discreetly sequestered on the third floor.

Every aspect of the design focuses on promoting superior care and a satisfactory patient experience. As John R. Detelich, CEO of Radiology Associates proudly says, "We offer a pleasant and friendly environment so that you can feel at ease when you visit our office."

Main entry

A. View of curved facade

B. Twilight view of building exterior

A

B

C

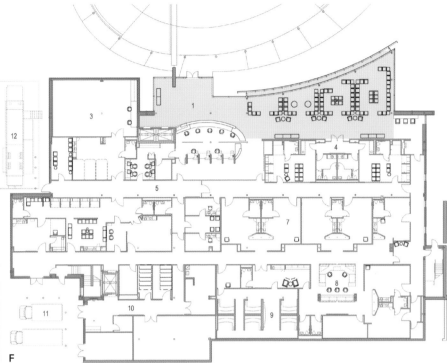

F

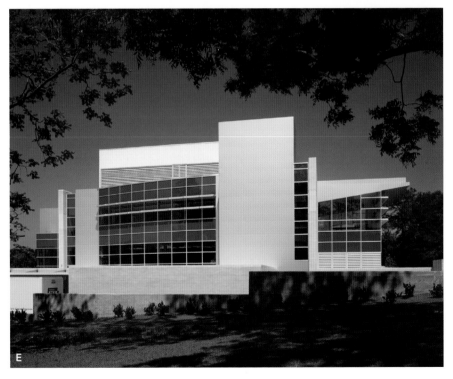

E

A. Main reception

B. Women's imaging reception

C. Main lobby

D. Canopy detail

E. West facade

F. First floor plan

CARDIOVASCULAR GROUP MEDICAL OFFICE BUILDING
Lawrenceville, Georgia

For all the headlines about Zika virus, Ebola, opioid addiction and other serious health hazards, 600,000 people die of heart disease in the United States every year, making it the nation's deadliest disease. Cardiovascular Group, in Gwinnett County, Georgia, is a consortium of 15 cardiologists that understands the impact of heart disease in metropolitan Atlanta. It commissioned Stanley Beaman & Sears to design its three-story, 30,500-square-foot medical office building in Lawrenceville to express the importance of treating and preventing cardiovascular disease and other ailments related to the heart and vascular system, and enhance the prominence of its practice among the professional buildings adjacent to Gwinnett Medical Center, to which it is affiliated.

The contemporary structure that houses the clinical and administrative offices and imaging center for the cardiologists and their support staffs easily commands attention with a sleek, curving architectural envelope of glass, metal and brick. The design's compelling imagery is more fully expressed inside. Because Stanley Beaman & Sears was given a relatively free hand in shaping the interiors, it chose the architecture of the heart itself as inspiration.

Just as the heart is organized as a symmetrical mirroring of chambers, the floor plan is arranged in a similar fashion. In form, color and texture, the interior design extends this concept through a layering of visual references to valve-like shapes and vascular flow. These references culminate in the vibrant warmth and saturation of the color palette. Evoking life, passion and joy, the design brings comfort and assurance to patients.

Main entry

E

A. Clinic corridor

B. Clinic entry

C. Lobby

D. Seating

E. Floor plans

UNIVERSITY OF CHICAGO
COMER CHILDREN'S HOSPITAL
Chicago, Illinois

An esteemed provider of comprehensive, innovative medical care to children since 1930, the University of Chicago Medicine set a formidable goal for its new, 155-bed, six-floor, 242,000-square-foot Comer Children's Hospital, designed by Stanley Beaman & Sears. The new facility would create an optimal setting for pediatric medicine's rapidly advancing technologies through architecture that would relate to the University's dignified campus, and interior design that would support children and their families. As the striking results show, Comer's designers met the challenge directly.

Thus, such advanced facilities as a 16-slice CT, state-of-the-art, network-linked patient bedside monitors, HEPA filtration of indoor air, a 30-bed PICU, a 55-bed NICU and six surgical suites with ORs exist alongside such child-centered features as patient rooms that accommodate family members and overnight stays, a Family Care Center with private sleeping rooms and bathrooms, laundry and vending machines, a Family Kitchen, a Family Learning Center, an outdoor playground with play equipment, and a Central Family Playroom on the ground floor.

No less noteworthy is Comer's contemporary architecture. Reinterpreting the University's Collegiate Gothic-style campus, the steel structure combines its glass curtain wall with pre-cast concrete columns and panels that constitute its solid and heavy base, inserting soaring steel "buttresses" to form a complex and dynamic form of overlapping masses that complements its campus neighbors. These bold forms are accompanied by fine details that express the respect for learning and the history of knowledge on campus. Subtle patterning in the pre-cast concrete panels appeals to a child's sense of discovery by recalling the large, elaborate and beautiful typeface characters found in many children's books, as well as the ivy that adorns many of the University's buildings. Another thoughtful feature is the building's metal panel "book ends," located on the two main stair towers at the north and south ends of the building.

The richness of the design has not escaped notice. Steve A. N. Goldstein, MD, PhD, chairman of the Department of Pediatrics and physician-in-chief of the Hospital, observes, "The University of Chicago Comer Children's Hospital is a remarkable synthesis of form and function."

Main entry and drop-off

A. Detail of canopy at main entry

B. Steel colonnade detail

C. Steel and precast detail

D. Canopy detail

A. West facede

B. Elevator tower

C. South facade

A. Main lobby

B. Main entry

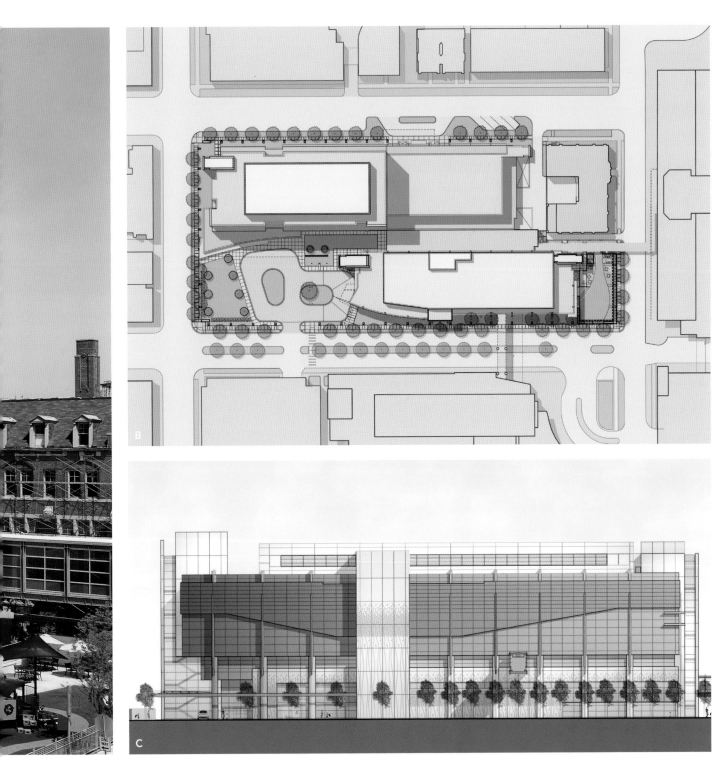

A. View of west facade

B. Precinct plan

C. West elevation

CHILDREN'S HEALTHCARE OF ATLANTA
Atlanta, Georgia

Formed in 1998 through the merger of Egleston Children's Health Care System and Scottish Rite Medical Center, Children's Healthcare of Atlanta traces its roots to the founding of Scottish Rite Convalescent Home for Crippled Children in 1915 and the opening of Henrietta Egleston Hospital for Children in 1928. Now comprising three hospitals and 27 urgent care centers and neighborhood clinics, Children's Healthcare is one of the nation's highest-rated children's hospitals. So when it launched the expansion and renovation of 255-bed Egleston Hospital (473,800 square feet) and 250-bed Scottish Rite Hospital (392,000 square feet), it asked the design team to consolidate dozens of specialty clinics and to introduce new and enlarged facilities within a family-friendly environment.

As patients and visitors happily discover, the new interiors introduce bright and playful spaces rich in nature-themed education and entertainment. Because the storytelling walls, murals and other special installations offer interactive and digital features, children relate to them enthusiastically, finding them as calming and therapeutic as they are engaging and distracting. Highlights include electronic feature walls in the main lobbies, video aquarium walls incorporating IMAX® film footage, Nadia's Room, a home-like facility easing patients' transition from hospital care, and the Stair Gym, a six-story staircase designed as a symbolic and therapeutic mountain climb.

Stanley Beaman & Sears has given Children's Healthcare of Atlanta, a long-term client, an effective healing environment based on what today's children truly want and need.

Discovery wall at public elevators

learning 2

through nature

Stigma
Style
Pistil
Ovary

The donor wall includes a **Leadership Club** listing with contributors organized by giving level:

Leadership Club
as of May 1, 2007

$10,000,000 PLUS
Anonymous (2)
Aflac Incorporated
Aflac Field Force
Children's Miracle Network

$5,000,000 PLUS
Mrs. Philip H. Alston
The Arthur M. Blank Family Foundation
Friends, the volunteer organization of
Children's Healthcare of Atlanta

$3,000,000 PLUS
Anonymous (1)
Kathelen and Dan Amos
Festival of Trees
The Carlos and Marguerite Mason Trust

$1,000,000 PLUS
Anonymous (3)
1998 Society - Physician Giving
Atlanta Classic Foundation
    Charities Inc.
BellSouth Corporation
Callaway Foundation Inc.
Children's Healthcare of Atlanta
    Employees
The Coca-Cola Company
Miriam H. and John A. Conant
CURE Childhood Cancer Inc.
Betty and Davis Fitzgerald Foundation
Thomas Egleston Trust
Trust Under Will of Frances B. Gable
Georgian Bank
Dr. and Mrs. Thomas K. Glenn II
The Kimberly and David Hanna
    Family Foundation
Kohl's Department Stores
Helen M. Kuechenmeister

The Marcus Foundation Inc.
The Robert W. Woodruff Foundation Inc.

The John H. Goddard Foundation Inc.
Lettie Pate Evans Foundation
Lettie Pate Evans Trust
Children's Healthcare of Atlanta
    Sports Network
News/Talk 750 WSB Care-a-Thon
Star 94 FM Cares for Kids Radiothon
Wachovia Bank
Wal-Mart/Sam's Club

Joseph P. Kuechenmeister
Forrest C. and Frances H. Lattner
    Foundation Inc.
Estate of Margaret Estelle Ledbetter
Marriott International
Irene McMath Trust
O. Wayne Rollins Foundation
Mr. and Mrs. Gary W. Rollins
Mr. and Mrs. R. Randall Rollins
Ms. Janet Sahr
Sibley Heart Center Cardiology
Patricia Bowman Terwilliger
    Family Foundation
Terwilliger Family Foundation
UPS Foundation
Waffle House Inc.
Estate of Eunice B. Weiss
Jesse Parker Williams
    Foundation
Nancy and John Williams
The Zeist Foundation

A. Video aquarium and donor wall

B. Public concourse and video totems

C. Dining

A. Main lobby

B. Public concourse

C. Emergency department

D. Patient registration

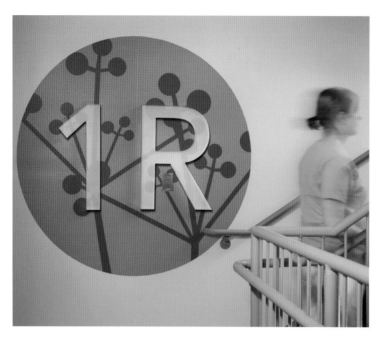

Stair gym

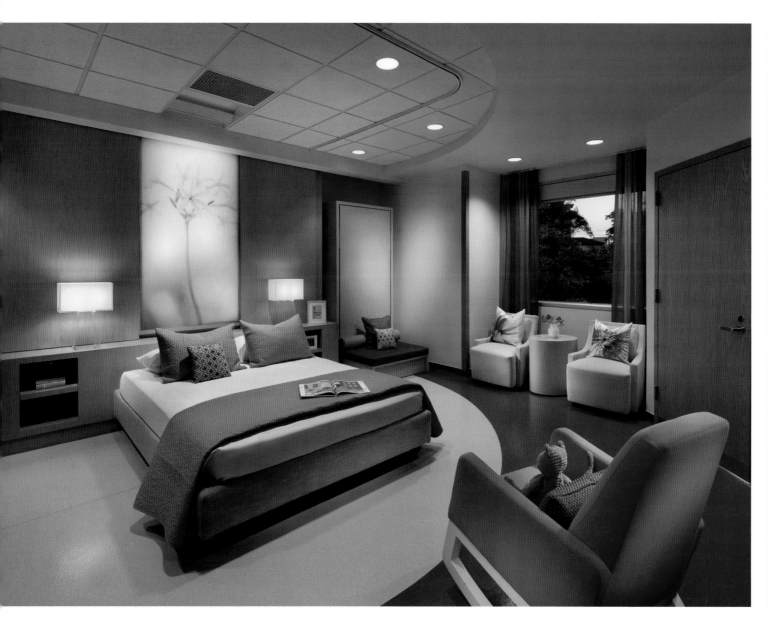

Nadia's room

ROOSEVELT WARM SPRINGS INSTITUTE FOR REHABILITATION
BLANCHARD HALL CENTER FOR ORTHOTICS AND PROSTHETICS
Warm Springs, Georgia

Poliomyelitis terrified American families in the first half of the 20th century, with major epidemics causing widespread paralysis and death in children and adults every summer from 1916. Having lost the use of his legs to polio as a young man, Franklin Delano Roosevelt traveled to the famed warm springs of Warm Springs, Georgia, for hydrotherapy, eventually establishing a treatment center for people with polio on the grounds of the springs in 1927. Now operated by the State of Georgia, the Roosevelt Warm Springs Institute for Rehabilitation has changed its mission considerably since Salk polio vaccine was successfully introduced in 1955, becoming a center for rehabilitation for all types of disabilities. A recent addition, the two-story, 35,000-square-foot Blanchard Hall Center for Orthotics and Prosthetics, designed by Stanley Beaman & Sears, opens a new gateway to the 1,700-acre campus.

Blanchard Hall accommodates clinics, fabrication workshops for orthotics and prosthetics, and a rehabilitation gymnasium in a building that respects the prevailing Classical Revival aesthetics of red brick and white colonnaded porticos and arcades through sympathetic scale, proportions and such details as its two-story entry lobby, portico and colonnade. However, it is strongly exemplifies contemporary architecture, re-imaging its historic neighbors using modern forms and such materials as steel, tensile fabric mesh and glass symbolic of some of the materials used for prosthetics.

Prominently set on a steep slope along the main road, the building connects to its parking area via a wheelchair-accessible bridge that does no damage to the warm spring beneath it, a timely symbol of the progressive approach to rehabilitation medicine practiced at Warm Springs.

Canopy at main entry

A. Main entry

B. Reception and lobby

A. Drop-off and colonnade

B. Exterior colonnade

C. Exterior detail

WEST VIRGINIA UNIVERSITY
ERMA BYRD BIOMEDICAL RESEARCH CENTER
Morgantown, West Virginia

Intensive, focused and stressful, the traditional science laboratory sheltered research teams that too frequently formed isolated, singularly-focused and self-contained communities. In developing the Erma Byrd Biomedical Research Center, West Virginia University envisioned a different research environment for its Morgantown campus. The four-level, 115,000-square-foot structure, designed by Stanley Beaman & Sears, would be an efficient, flexible laboratory that would encourage collaboration and cross-disciplinary exchange among researchers and students, and serve as an architectural landmark to attract prestigious investigators and projects.

To accomplish this, the design separates activities into distinct linear zones where researchers and students enjoy daily contact. Open bay laboratories, fixed modules that can adapt to multiple modes of research, are aligned along the west side of each floor. Offices, ranging from researchers' private spaces with transparent interior walls to post-doctoral students' open desks, conference rooms, and areas for informal assembly occupy the east side. Between these is a layered axis consisting of a ghost corridor housing laboratory sinks, a file of alcoves for support activities and equipment, and a security wall finished on the office side with custom millwork and opaque blue art-glass "windows."

The contemporary interiors are enriched by bright colors, wood paneling, sturdy yet comfortable furnishings, and a nuanced lighting design aided by windows bringing natural light and outdoor views indoors. Outside, the precisely machined but angular geometry of the glass-and-steel façade represents a striking departure from the restrained Modernism of the University's Morgantown campus, announcing a new era in the University's expanding mission in research.

Twilight view of east facade

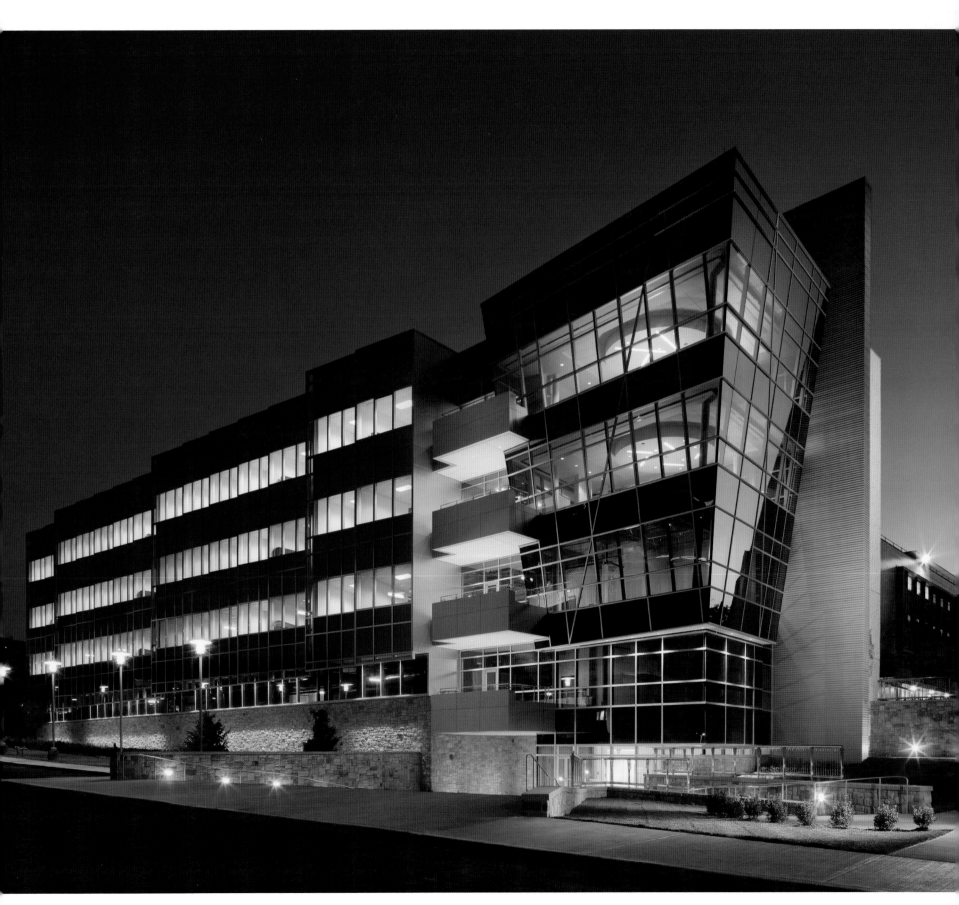

A. Collaboration space and feature wall

B. Principal investigators' conferencing center

A

A. Building elevation at principal investigators' offices

B. Detail view of conference rooms on each levels

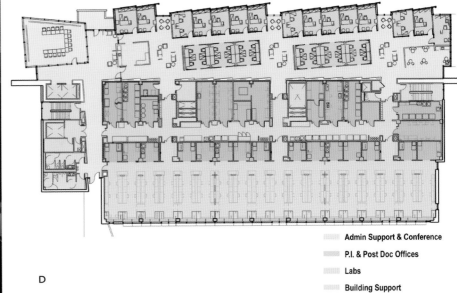

- Admin Support & Conference
- P.I. & Post Doc Offices
- Labs
- Building Support

D

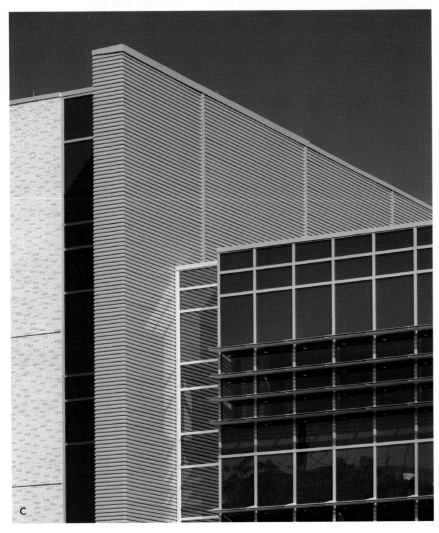

A. Facade detail

B. Typical research lab

C. Facade detail

D. Typical floor plan

KENNEDY KRIEGER INSTITUTE
HARRY AND JEANETTE WEINBERG CENTER FOR DEVELOPMENTAL DISABILITIES
Baltimore, Maryland

An oasis of hope and confidence for children and adolescents with brain and spinal cord difficulties--and an affirmation for the staff serving them-- has opened in Baltimore: the Harry and Jeanette Weinberg Center for Developmental Disabilities, the outpatient center of Kennedy Krieger Institute. Outpatient services at Kennedy Krieger, an affiliate of Johns Hopkins School of Medicine dedicated to research, education and therapeutic care for children with neurological injuries and developmental disabilities, were previously housed in scattered locations. The award-winning, six-story, 115,000-square-foot facility, designed by Stanley Beaman & Sears with the participation of patients, families and staff, consolidates these services in a therapeutic environment that seamlessly integrates building, interior and landscape.

Inside, such essential facilities as 40 examination rooms, therapy pools, physical therapy and spinal cord therapy gyms, sensory integration gym, multi-functional OT/PT/speech/audiology/ADL suite, and conference center are introduced through the expansive, two-story lobby, where organic shapes, nature-themed colors and touch-inviting materials extend a soothing welcome. Outside, the contemporary architecture advances the Center's mission by using its glass walls and curving masses to capture daylight and views as they showcase its work to the city, while the block-long therapeutic garden, organized into distinct "rooms" devoted to mobility activities for young patients and respite for families and staff, simultaneously respects the need for privacy and proclaims the Center's presence.

Conceived as a three-part process, the design expresses therapy in its form and mass, research in its curtain wall, and hope in its transparency, a message that the new Center eloquently conveys.

Exterior view of entry and lobby

A. Main entry

B. View from therapy garden

A. Main reception

B. Lobby

C. Registration

A. Second floor lobby

B. Therapy pools

C. Registration and check-in

D. Clinical zone

E. Exterior view of facade

A. Therapy garden

B. View from garden

PIEDMONT PHYSICIANS GROUP
Atlanta, Georgia

The more than 150 primary care doctors and 50 specialists of Piedmont Physicians Group, a multi-disciplinary practice affiliated with Piedmont Healthcare, one of Atlanta's leading healthcare providers since 1905, have witnessed countless demonstrations of the impact that the healthcare environment can have on patient outcomes. So when Piedmont Physicians commissioned Stanley Beaman & Sears to design a new, one-floor, 5,000 square-foot physicians' office in Midtown, Atlanta's most dynamic district, it requested a setting to express its belief in "Healthcare without Complexities." In essence, the physicians wanted the space to support their patient-focused philosophy, using basic compositional elements made from quality materials to support a patient experience that would be appealing, uncomplicated and reassuring.

With the Group's vision of excellence in mind, the design team established a design vocabulary characterized by simplicity of plane, line, material and color – echoing the principles of reduction essential to the modernist aesthetic--and a material palette comprising attractive and durable building products and interior furnishings. The result is a carefully constructed and finely tailored setting where purity, serenity and contemporary urbanity surround the patient. For example, the ceiling heights range from nine to over ten feet, allowing natural light and outdoor views to be maximized, and keeping patients in visual contact with the outside world.

Every interior detail, from recessed magazine holders, soap dispensers and coat hooks to crisp colors, subtle architectural lighting and gallery artwork, projects the same high level of concern. "Healthcare without Complexities" thus becomes a visible reality for healthcare and design alike.

Clinic corridor

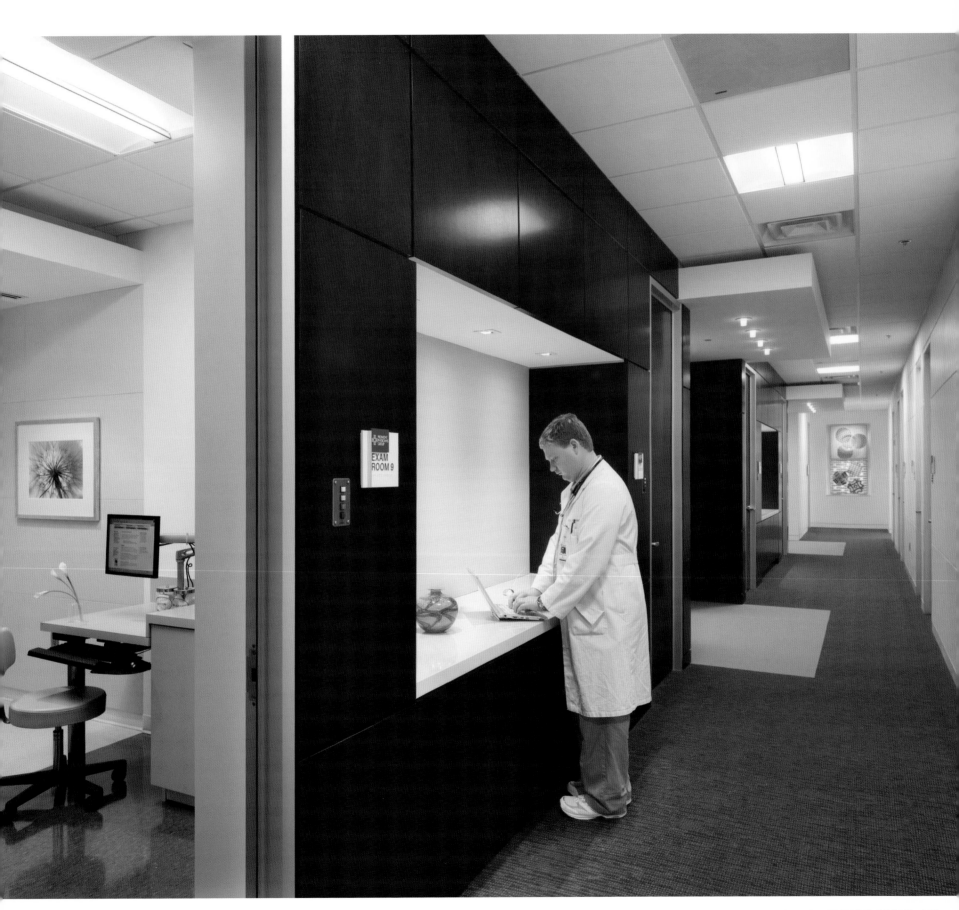

Clinic corridor

Reception and check-in

Family waiting

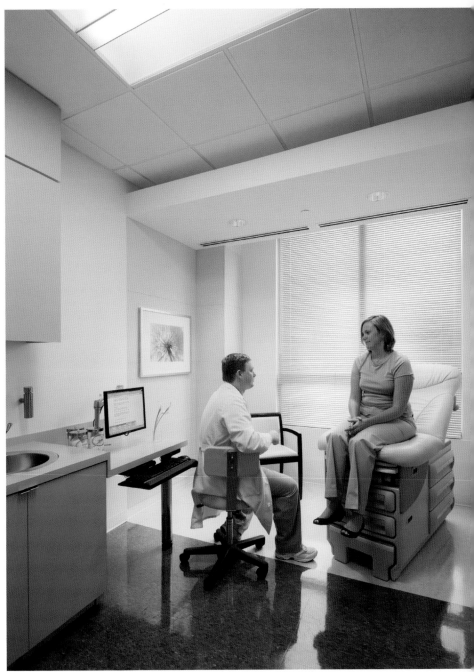

Typical exam room

GEORGIA INSTITUTE OF TECHNOLOGY
Atlanta, Georgia

Many colleges install traditional low brick walls and horizontal signs at campus entrances, but Georgia Institute of Technology retained Stanley Beaman & Sears to design something different for its 400-acre Atlanta campus: contemporary campus gateway monument signage. More like digital icons than piles of masonry, the sleek, oval-shaped vertical signs in silver metal mark Georgia Tech's presence in the community, offer flexibility for relocation, and confer a progressive, high-tech image. The project's success gave Stanley Beaman & Sears the larger assignment to provide wayfinding and environmental graphic signage services for the entire campus.

The impact of the campus-wide commission is unmistakable at Clough Undergraduate Learning Commons, a five-story, 220,000-square-foot academic building that houses facilities for first- and second-year students and doubles as a student commons. Here, environmental graphics, wayfinding and donor recognition reflect the building's advanced design and technology, as well as the digital world students inhabit. Since open, flexible spaces and more reactive and less linear educational experiences are increasingly favored, the design team turned to such environments as airports and ground transportation stations, where destinations are delivered quickly and intelligibly, for inspiration.

As a result, directional signage occupies elevated positions, and floor plans resemble transit maps. Colors, materials and visual symbols also convey strategic information. Georgia Tech's blue and gold define the corridors, for example, signage along the west wall uses resin panels to transmit daylight, and fields of study are represented by corresponding motifs on resin panels and interior windows, such as a caffeine molecule for chemistry.

Monumental gateway signs

A

B

The sign reads:

230-270

Restrooms
Breakout Rooms
Grand Stair & Elevators
You Are Here

→

WEST

classrooms

TENNENBAUM ATRIUM

C

A. Monumental gateway signs

B. Physics lab signage

C. Main directional signage

A. Signage detail

B. Typical classroom / lab signage

C. Main lobby directional signage

D. Third floor directional signage

ADAMSVILLE REGIONAL HEALTH CENTER
Atlanta, Georgia

Opened in 2012 to address the healthcare and social needs of an economically challenged, predominantly African-American population, Adamsville Regional Health Center was designed by Stanley Beaman & Sears for Fulton County, Georgia to serve Adamsville, an urban neighborhood on Atlanta's west side at the intersection of Interstate 20 and Interstate 285. Its welcoming presence is unmistakable. The two-story, 36,000-sq. ft. structure delineates the northeast edge of a four-acre site bordering Martin Luther King Jr. Drive, an arterial thoroughfare, giving it visibility to people arriving by private car and public transportation or on foot. It was fast-tracked, designed and constructed in 275 days, and garnered LEED certification and an American Institute of Architects/ Academy for Health Design Award.

A holistic concept of wellness makes the Center especially convenient and effective. By co-locating a primary care clinic, behavioral health clinic, childcare facilities, a dental clinic and workforce community center under its sheltering, cantilevered roof, it makes visits convenient and economical for patients of varied backgrounds and conditions. The spatial organization, anchored by a central, two-story lobby and connecting stair, easily guides visitors to their destinations. Likewise, the attractive, quilt-like exterior metal paneling, inspired by the paintings of Atlanta artist Radcliff Bailey, celebrates the cultural roots of Adamsville residents.

Other on-site amenities transcend basic utility. A drop-in childcare center assists parents receiving services. A community garden supervised by a master gardener promotes exercise and nutrition. And a colorful indoor play area helps families to relieve stress by letting children do what comes naturally.

Northwest entrance

A. Main lobby

B. Connecting stair

C. First-floor corridor

South elevation

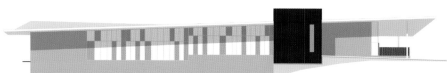

North elevation

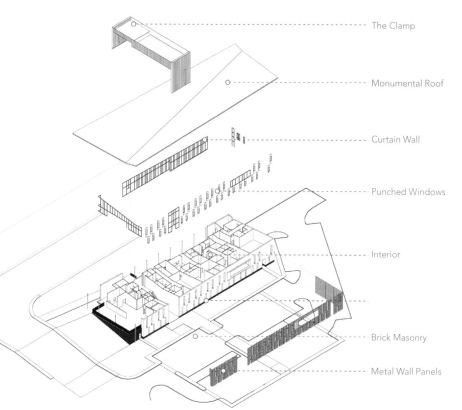

The Clamp

Monumental Roof

Curtain Wall

Punched Windows

Interior

Brick Masonry

Metal Wall Panels

South elevation

A. Detail clinic

B. Atrium

C. View of west elevation

NEMOURS CHILDREN'S HOSPITAL
Orlando, Florida

Alfred I. duPont (1864-1935) was determined to improve the lives of sick children, leading to the formation of The Nemours Foundation in 1936 and the Alfred I. duPont Institute, a pediatric orthopedic hospital in Wilmington, Delaware, in 1940. An ambitious, 21st-century expression of his concern is the 95-bed, six-story, 630,000-square-foot Nemours Children's Hospital in Orlando, designed by Stanley Beaman & Sears, design architect and architect of record.

Nemours brings a new level of pediatric healthcare to Central Florida with all private patient rooms, pediatric emergency department, NICU, PICU, Nemours Children's Clinic, and extensive research and education facilities. It is more than a showcase for new technology, state-of-the-art equipment, innovative building materials, lighting and interactive features. Because it aligns outpatient and inpatient care within a single facility, outpatient clinics and inpatient rooms for specific medical specialties occupy adjacent wings of the same floor with shared waiting spaces, letting children become familiar with care teams during both clinic visits and inpatient stays.

Medical staff, administrators, parents and children participated in Nemours's design. The result is a unique healing environment. Such details as private patient rooms with overnight accommodations, laundry facilities, concierge desks in patient-floor elevator lobbies, family lounges, playrooms, landscaped rooftop terraces, interactive water features, one-acre "discovery garden" and outdoor community stage for live performances--plus such amenities as a gift shop, café, and on-site pharmacy--demonstrate why children and families feel inspired and empowered here.

Nemours is also one of three Florida children's hospitals to achieve LEED Gold certification. To balance energy consumption with occupant comfort--a major concern in promoting sustainability--the design team focused on controlling the region's intense sun and high humidity. Extensive solar studies supported the creation of shaded outdoor spaces and sunscreens that block direct sunlight while admitting natural light indoors. Coupled with proper building orientation and the use of green roofs, these measures provide energy savings of 22 percent and improve the operating efficiency of building mechanical systems without compromising comfort.

The building's modern architecture reinforces the high-tech, high-touch environment inside. Pre-cast concrete, metal panels, warm-colored terracotta clay tiles and metal panels framing the building's three entry portals) give the façade an image of sleek form tempered by warm color. Being timeless and in harmony with other clinical and research buildings at the Medical City in Lake Nona, a mixed-use planned community, Nemours supports children indoors and out.

Main entry

A-D. Architectural details

E. Patient drop-off

E

A. North facade and event lawn

B. Event lawn and community stage

C. Interactive water feature

A. Main lobby and reception   B. Interactive feature   D. KidsTrack

C. Main entry   E. Dining

A

B

C

D

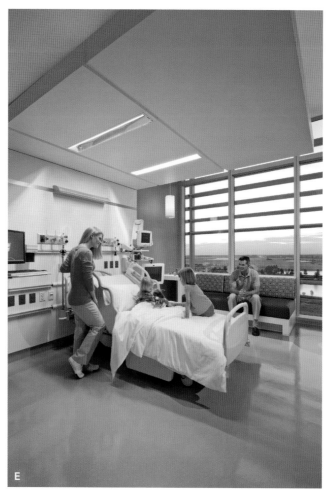

E

F

A. Clinic waiting

B. Outpatient center

C. Emergency department

D. Chapel

E. Patient room

F. Typical elevator lobby

G. Conference center pre-function area

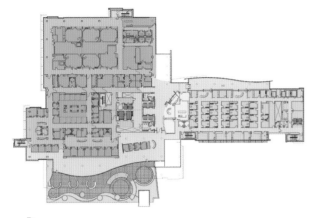

B

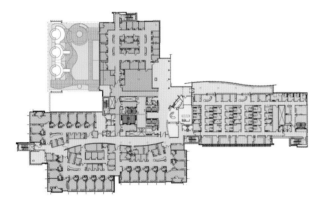

C

A. Emergency entrance

B. Perioperative floor and surgical clinics

C. Inpatient / Outpatient / Hemotology / Oncology floor plan

D. Second floor surgery roof garden

D

BAPTIST MEDICAL CENTER
WOLFSON CHILDREN'S HOSPITAL
Jacksonville, Florida

The opening of the 11-story, 300,000-square-foot J. Wayne and Delores Barr Weaver Tower on the Baptist Medical Center campus in Jacksonville, Florida, designed by Stanley Beaman & Sears, marks an important milestone for Wolfson Children's Hospital, a 216-bed institution founded in 1955. Wolfson is critical to the healthcare of its growing region, providing North Florida, South Georgia and the Florida Panhandle their only full-service tertiary pediatric hospital. The new tower expands existing facilities on the downtown campus for Baptist Jacksonville Hospital as well as Wolfson, an institution praised as one of America's Best Children's Hospitals by U.S. News & World Report.

In the lower half of the tower occupied by Wolfson, the facilities include pediatric cardiovascular intensive care, operating suites that permit MRI and CT scans during surgery, and more patient beds, along with a neurological operating room and neurological intensive care for children and adults. Wolfson's interiors represent a very special place, as children promptly discover. To exploit the strong relationship between environment and clinical outcomes, Stanley Beaman & Sears developed special nature motifs for every floor. Featuring rivers, forests and grasslands inspired by nearby natural habitats, the motifs shape the interiors through large, colorful and dramatic passive and interactive graphics.

This life-affirming vision extends into patient rooms. Sized 100 square feet bigger than existing counterparts, the new accommodations are all family suites with full bathrooms, refrigerators, safes and daybeds. Not only do they feel more like homes than hospitals, children happily find they have their own animal themes. Their windows, shielded by exterior horizontal sunscreens along the south-facing curtainwall to offer shade and save energy, bring spectacular views of the St. John's River and an abundance of natural light to further lift their spirits.

South elevation

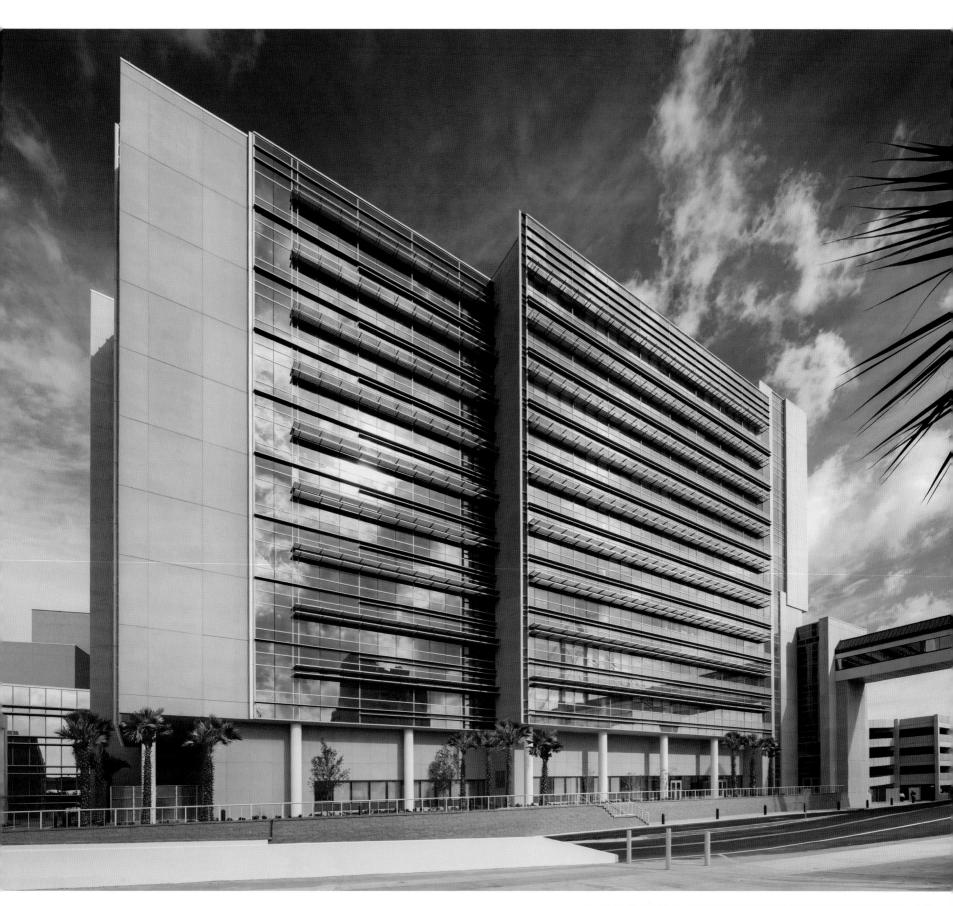

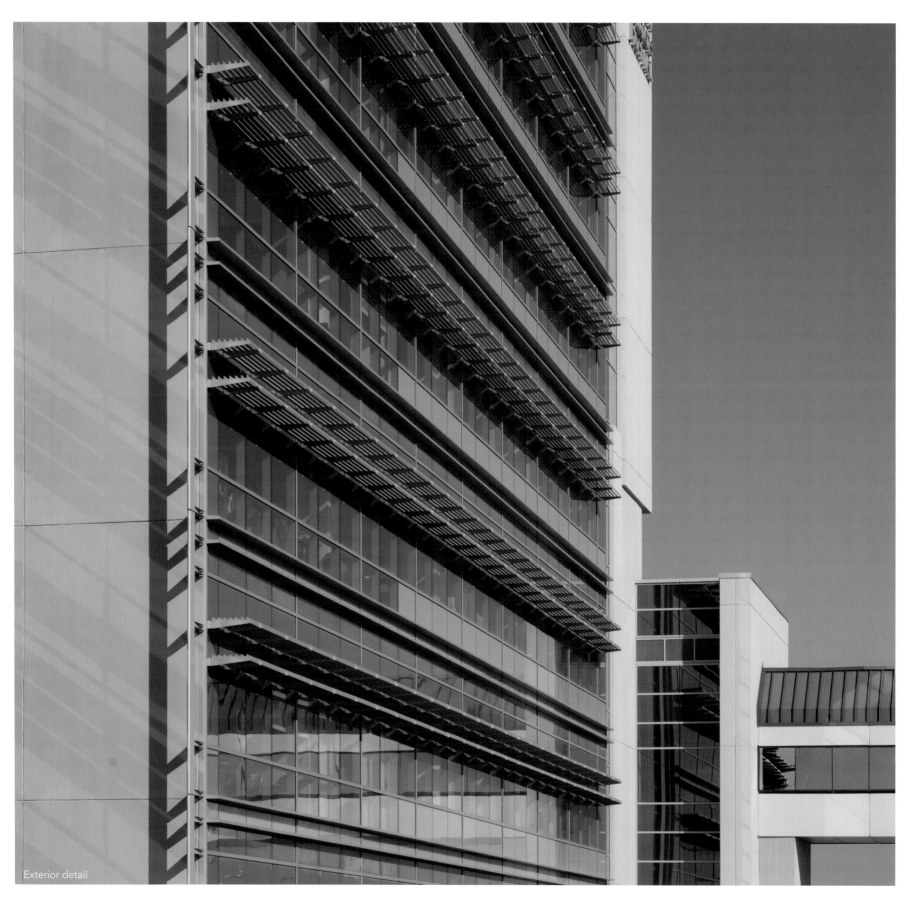

Exterior detail

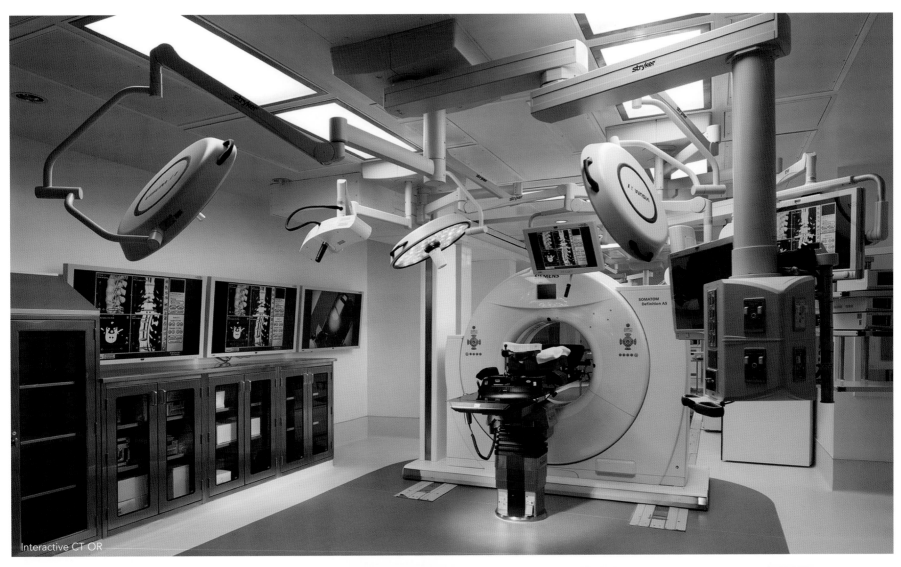

Interactive CT OR

Elevator lobby and educational feature

Public corridor

A. Clinical zone

B. Typical patient room

C. Educational feature wall

D. Patient greeter

E. Video wall

UNIVERSITY HOSPITALS / RAINBOW BABIES & CHILDREN'S ANGIE FOWLER ADOLESCENT & YOUNG ADULT CANCER INSTITUTE

Cleveland, Ohio

Unhappy adolescent and young adult (AYA) cancer patients often find that pediatric and adult oncology fail to meet their medical and social needs, which differ from those of infants, younger children and adults. The Angie Fowler Adolescent & Young Adult Cancer Institute of University Hospitals Rainbow Babies & Children's Hospital, at Cleveland Medical Center in downtown Cleveland, was designed by Stanley Beaman & Sears to resolve this dilemma. In renovating the eighth floor to create the 18,500-square-foot Institute, and converting the ninth floor rooftop into the 7,500-square-foot Angie's Garden, the design team worked closely with medical staff, patients, families and the primary donor, the Fowler family, whose daughter Angie succumbed to melanoma.

Developing an outpatient program for AYA patients was complex and technical, but the resulting environment has been effective in treating patients and attracting top cancer researchers and physicians. Stanley Beaman & Sears developed the space as a "journey of light and healing" that leads the patient through "zones of interaction." Typically, the patient follows the 60-foot-long illuminated "welcome wall" from the lobby to one of two treatment wings and a decentralized care team station adjacent to treatment and examination rooms, with possible stops at various waiting areas, consultation and meeting rooms, a teen lounge and a pharmacy.

Angie's Garden, by contrast, feels magical. With a variety of trees, herbs, flowers and other plantings, colorful animal sculptures and multiple seating areas, the rooftop healing garden lets patients and families escape from the clinical environment without actually leaving it. That's magic, by design.

Main reception and welcome wall

Interactive Wall

A

A. Teen lounge

B. Learning zone

C. Interactive welcome wall

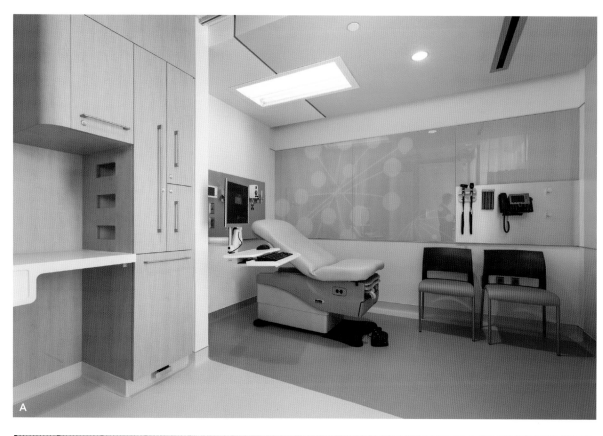

A. Typical exam room

B. Consult room

C. family waiting area

Eco wall and roof garden

GALLERY 72
Atlanta, Georgia

Solid buildings with "good bones" can lead multiple lives. Because the former home of the Atlanta Journal Constitution in downtown Atlanta, 72 Marietta Street NW, had been reduced to a single tenant, the City of Atlanta's Department of Watershed Management, the City moved decisively to revive what real estate professionals call its "curb appeal."
As a part of international design competition, a commission was awarded to Stanley Beaman & Sears by Atlanta's Office of Cultural Affairs to renovate the eight-story, pre-cast concrete structure by introducing a fascia that glows against the existing façade and flows directly into the building, along with a remodeled, 3,400-square-foot ground-floor space.

The linking of façade and ground-floor interior to draw pedestrians inside is accomplished by stretching a broad, ribbon-like form some 2,500 feet from the back wall of the entrance lobby across the lobby ceiling, through the vestibule, and out to the entry plaza, where the form acts like a marquee in an abrupt, 90-degree turn and vertical ascent of the building's south façade. Evoking the movement of paper through newspaper printing presses in its dynamic twists and turns, the expressionistic form provides a lively contrast with the building's static grid of pre-cast panels.

Inside, the design provides a futuristic entrance lobby flanked by two flexible gallery spaces on either side, the North and South Galleries, that are fully visible from the street and sidewalk. Whatever the future holds for the building and its surrounding neighborhood, the design has brought fresh energy and vision to the building now called 2 City Plaza.

Main entry marquee

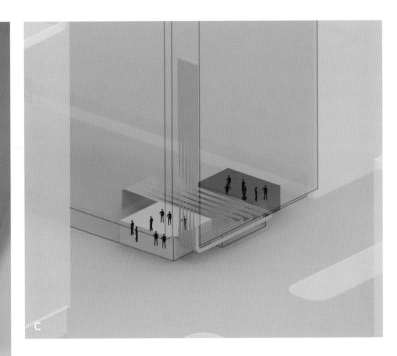

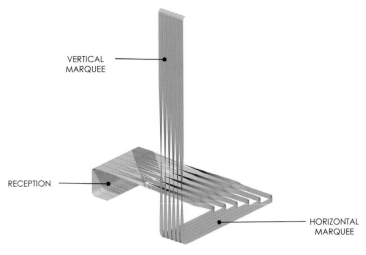

VERTICAL
MARQUEE

RECEPTION

HORIZONTAL
MARQUEE

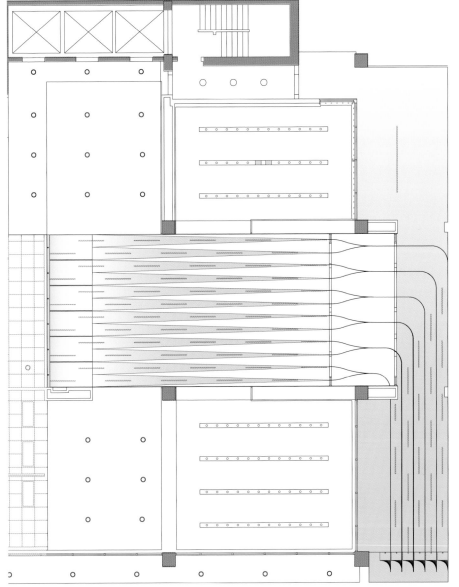

A. Exterior view of vertical marquee

B. Main lobby reception

C. Axonometric rendering and plan diagram

A. 2 City Plaza marquee

B. South gallery

KENNESAW STATE UNIVERSITY
BERNARD A. ZUCKERMAN MUSEUM OF ART
Kennesaw, Georgia

An unlikely cultural center has emerged in Kennesaw, Georgia, 25 miles northwest of Atlanta, on the campus of Kennesaw State University: the Bernard A. Zuckerman Museum of Art. The two-story, 9,200-square-foot contemporary building, designed by Stanley Beaman & Sears, not only brought the first art museum to a campus of the University System of Georgia in over 30 years--KSU, founded as a junior college in 1966, is now Georgia's third-largest public institution of higher education--it spurred the growth of a new cultural district in greater Atlanta. This was goal from the beginning, when KSU and Bernard A. Zuckerman, an industrialist and philanthropist, began the initiative to build a stand-alone museum uniting the university's permanent art collection with its campus galleries program.

Although the building emerges from the side of a hill crowned by the much larger mass of the adjacent Bailey Performance Center, the museum boldly asserts itself with its striking black and white façade. Rotated off-axis, it directly addresses a main vehicular entry to the campus, heralding KSU's new "Arts District." The two-story glass atrium, highlighting the public circulation space and entrance, stands at the corner of the building, conveniently close to the parking lot and primary pedestrian path. The entrance, marked by an unobtrusive awning created by a subtle outward cant of the façade, takes advantage of being connected to its neighbor by doubling as an extended reception and pre-function space for Bailey's 624-seat auditorium.

The exterior materials foreshadow the interior's straightforward arrangement. Most of the façade at ground level consists of black concrete block, lending a sense of stability and rigidity to the edifice, to appropriately enclose the storage and support spaces. The second floor, which contains the gallery space, is veiled in light white metal panels, contrasting sharply with the heavy massing below. The parapet is crenellated in a pattern based on the Fibonacci sequence, adding texture while paying homage to the mathematical phenomena in nature, visual art and music.

In addition to changing exhibitions, the museum is the venue of KSU's significant collection of sculpture by Ruth Zuckerman, Mr. Zuckerman's late wife. Many of these pieces can be viewed by visitors passing through the gardens surrounding the arts complex. Like the museum itself, they encourage the university's 33,000 students and the public to participate in the region's vibrant cultural life.

Main entry view

A-B. East galleries

Building detail

Entry with canopy

Ruth Zuckerman pavilion

Ruth Zuckerman pavilion

UNIVERSITY OF VIRGINIA HEALTH SYSTEM
BATTLE BUILDING
Charlottesville, Virginia

For generations, the gateway to the University of Virginia in Charlottesville has been Thomas Jefferson's iconic Rotunda and Lawn. Now, the university also has a 21st-century gateway, the Battle Building, part of the University of Virginia Children's Hospital at the University of Virginia Medical Center. The seven-story, 200,300-square-foot structure, designed by Stanley Beaman & Sears, interior architect and interior designer, has two distinct tenants: the UVA Outpatient Surgery Center, with 12 ORs serving both adults and pediatrics, and all of UVA Children's Hospital's outpatient clinics. To help children and families navigate the facility, floors are organized to simplify wayfinding based on references to the geography of UVA and Charlottesville, and facilities are designed with storytelling themes to engage children, using static displays and interactive features highlighting such classic children's books as "Charlotte's Web," "Curious George" and "The Jungle Book." Even the 75 examination rooms display lively storybook silhouettes.

All 36 specialty clinics are organized in interdisciplinary, multifunctional "neighborhoods" for care, with complimentary clinics conveniently co-located so multiple caregivers can go to patients, rather than ask patients to go to multiple clinics. In addition, there are such thoughtful accommodations as waiting rooms located along "Main Street," 40-foot-long interactive storytelling walls in each of the four upper-floor waiting rooms, and family activity areas for storytelling and play. All pediatric facilities are entirely focused on children and families.

The scale of children and the joy of discovery and storytelling are powerful sources of visual vocabulary that repeatedly invigorate the design. A green feature wall and a wood-clad main elevator bank symbolizing a treehouse take children to magical worlds conceptually and physically. A playspace on each floor, sporting its own, exclusive color scheme, provides a safe and inviting environment for the children and a colorful illuminated beacon visible to the neighborhood at night. While the LEED Gold certified Battle Building cannot guarantee that every patient's story will end happily ever after, it gives children joy, enlightenment and hope.

Main entry view

A

A. Main lobby and reception

B. Donor recognition

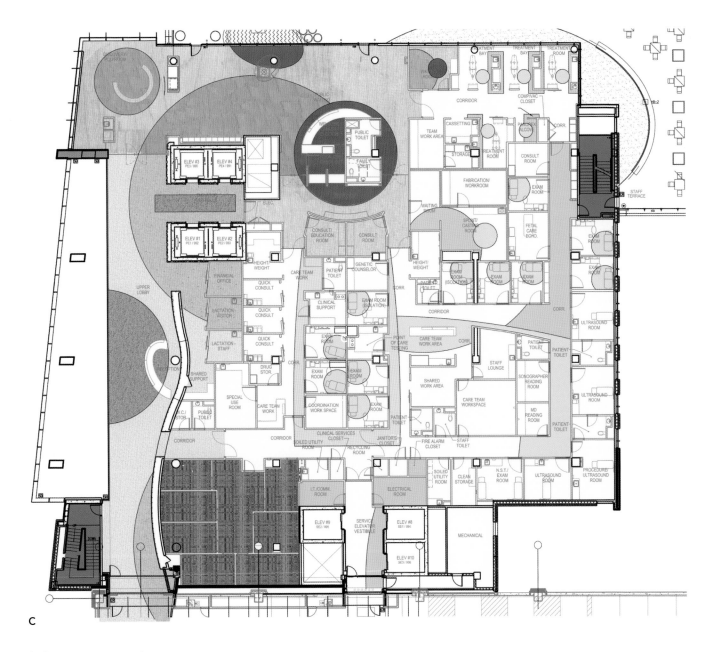

C

A. Surgery center reception

B. Surgery center registration and waiting

C. Typical clinic floor plan

Family activity area

Interactive story-telling wall

Custom children's book educational I Spy graphics in each exam room

CHILDREN'S HOSPITAL OF SAN ANTONIO

San Antonio, Texas

Thanks to the Sisters of Charity of the Incarnate Word, who founded Santa Rosa Infirmary, San Antonio's first hospital, in 1869, Children's Hospital of San Antonio opened as the city's first children's hospital in 1959. Fifty-three years later, Christus Santa Rosa Health System received approval from Christus Health to convert its 11-story, 400,000-square-foot downtown facility into San Antonio's first freestanding children's hospital. Stanley Beaman & Sears was named the hospital's interior designer, due to its expertise in pediatric design, joining WHR as architect of record and Overland Partners as exterior architect.

Patients and their families immediately feel welcome at the new Children's Hospital of San Antonio. Wayfinding is straightforward, anchored by a stunning new lobby featuring a circular chapel. Other interiors are likewise accessible and distinctive, adopting "The Spirit of the River" as a theme to create impressions of San Antonio's well-known "River Walk" and the Christus Health System's missionary history. Alluding to the therapeutic qualities of water, hope and faith in the healing process, the hospital presents a wide array of wonderfully sculpted spaces illuminated by halos of light and enriched with design elements rooted in San Antonio's heritage.

From the lobby to accommodations including a dedicated ER for children, 12 pediatric surgery ORs, 200 private patient rooms where parents can stay overnight, and such amenities as play rooms, family gathering rooms and family break rooms offering dining, TV and laundry facilities, the hospital embraces all that is near and dear to children and families of San Antonio.

Main lobby and chapel

Chapel entry and monumental stair

Chapel

Chapel detail

Chapel ceiling detail

Entry drop-off

Reception / greeter desk

Dining room

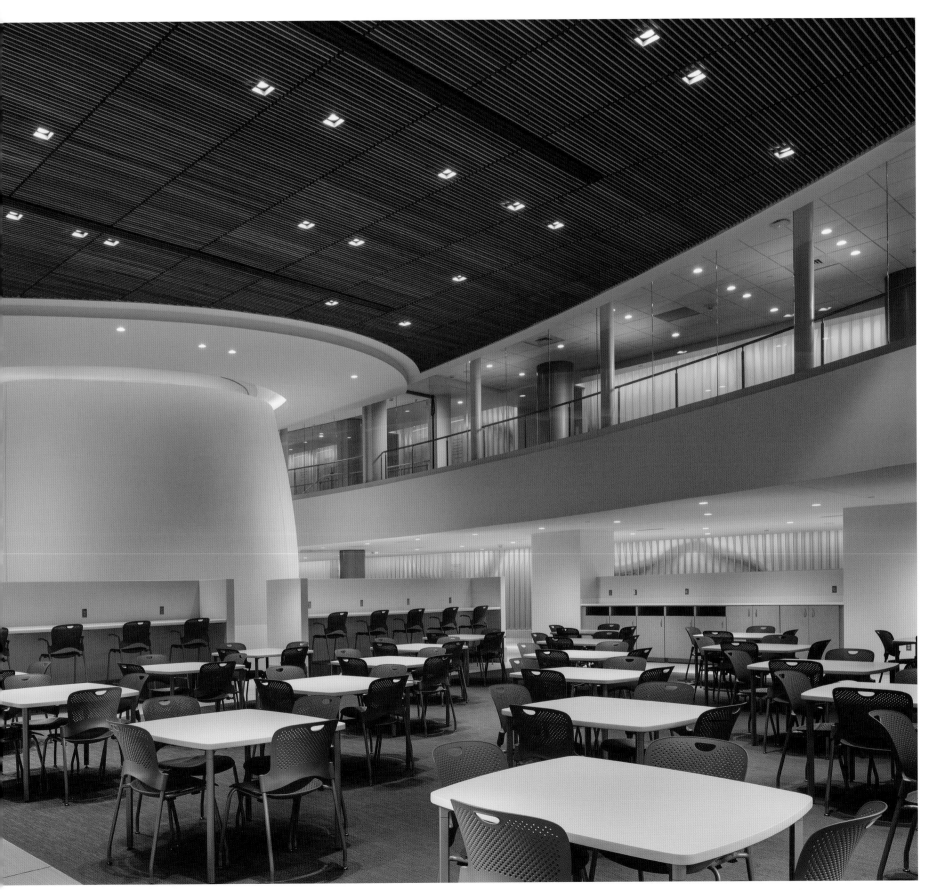

ATLANTA CONTEMPORARY ART CENTER
Atlanta, Georgia

Established as an artists' cooperative in 1973, Atlanta Contemporary has become one of the Southeast's leading contemporary art centers. As a non-profit, non-collecting institution, located in Atlanta's West Midtown district, it is dedicated to the creation, presentation, and advancement of contemporary art by emerging and established artists. Besides presenting six to ten exhibitions annually, it is one of a few Atlanta institutions that commissions new work from artists. Its home, a renovated, 35,000-square-foot warehouse complex housing exhibition galleries and studios for working artists near the campus of Georgia Institute of Technology, recently embarked on a long-term institutional planning project.

The absence of a true physical "core," or center between The Contemporary's existing buildings inspired a series of formal studies that examined ways that a genuine "heart" could be created. Studies by Stanley Beaman & Sears examined how two major program components, The Contemporary's existing large gallery space and a new 250-seat theater for IMAGE Film and Video, could anchor each end of the site and constitute a dynamic form when viewed from the neighborhood's major thoroughfare, Marietta Street Artery. Two dominant curved forms emerged, beginning at the front entry and concluding in the proposed performance space and video theatre, to introduce a much-needed visual connection throughout the site and facilities, as well as flexible indoor and outdoor spaces for a variety of programs.

The master site and facilities studies strongly suggest that The Contemporary and IMAGE could jointly position themselves as a flourishing vanguard destination in Atlanta for years to come.

Floor plan, section and model studies

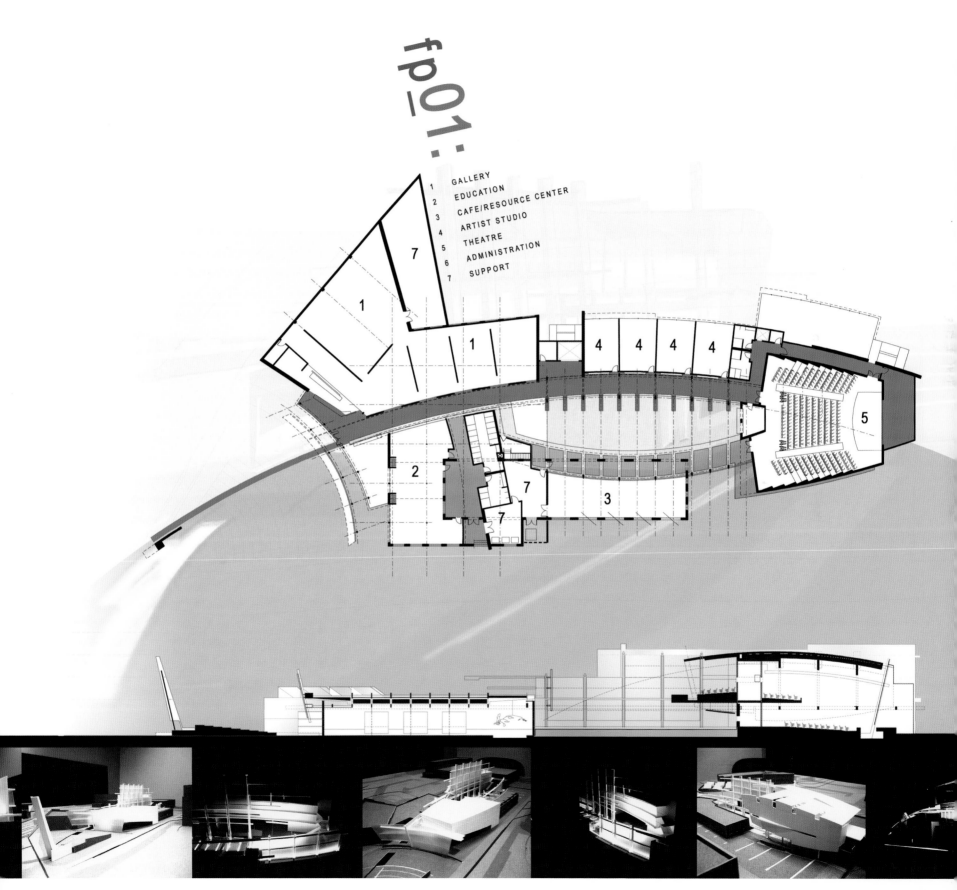

fp 01:

1 GALLERY
2 EDUCATION
3 CAFE/RESOURCE CENTER
4 ARTIST STUDIO
5 THEATRE
6 ADMINISTRATION
7 SUPPORT

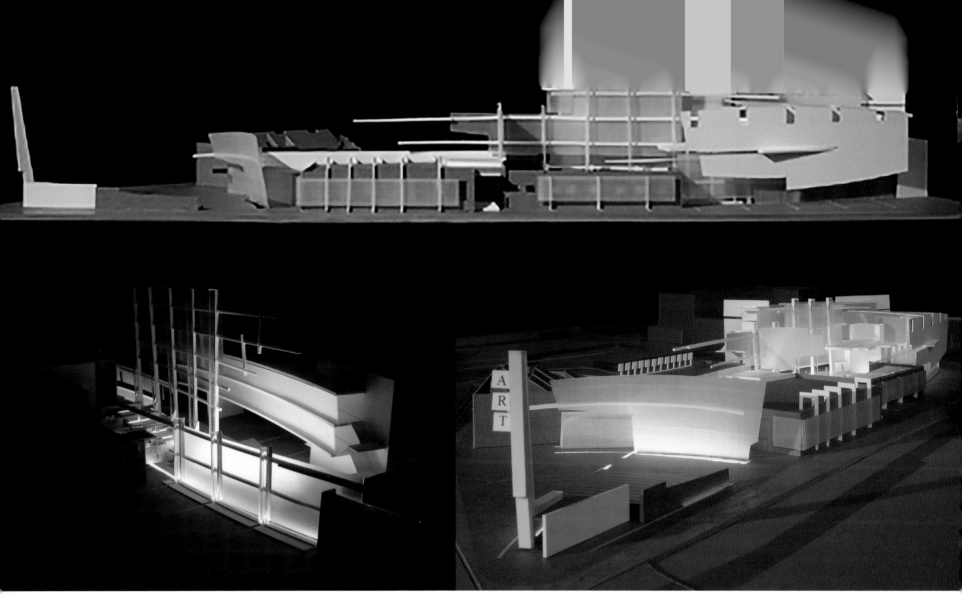

Model studies

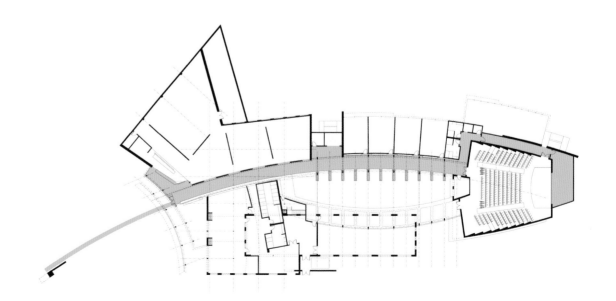

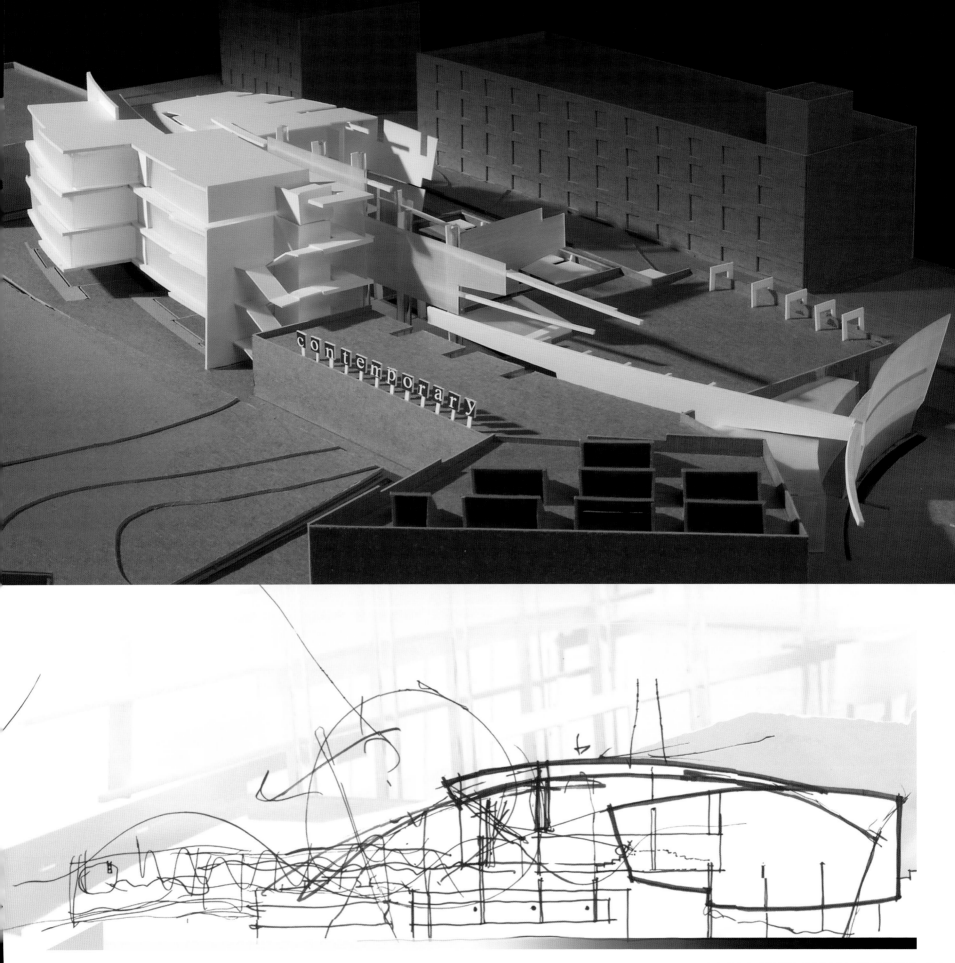

ATLANTA HISTORY CENTER
Atlanta, Georgia

If the Smithsonian Institution is termed "the nation's attic" because of its eclectic holdings of some 138 million items, the Atlanta History Center could easily be called "Atlanta's attic." A history museum and research center founded in 1926, the Atlanta History Center currently showcases six permanent and several temporary exhibitions and one of the nation's largest collections of Civil War artifacts on a 33-acre campus in the Buckhead district that includes historic houses and gardens. Like many venerable institutions, however, the Atlanta History Center modified and enlarged its original home of 1926 to the extent that its spaces and circulation became badly disconnected. Stanley Beaman & Sears won second place in the Center's international design competition to update its architecture and interior design with a highly regarded 30,000-square-foot renovation and expansion.

Under the wing-like roof of a new Hall of Enlightenment, the design established a clear spatial hierarchy to unite the existing lobby, exhibition galleries, and ballroom pre-function or overlook space. Cross-section panels allowed displays to emerge and vanish into the spaces between the ribs while concealing necessary building systems suspended from a space framing system above. Other key features of the design included a Knowledge Hub, with its interactive display engine to orient visitors and reveal the vast array of museum offers, and Discovery Portals, learning cores engaging multi-generational audiences in active learning, discovery and research.

In effect, the re-imagined Center turned the casual spectator into an active participant in the city's colorful story of past, present and future.

View of main entry

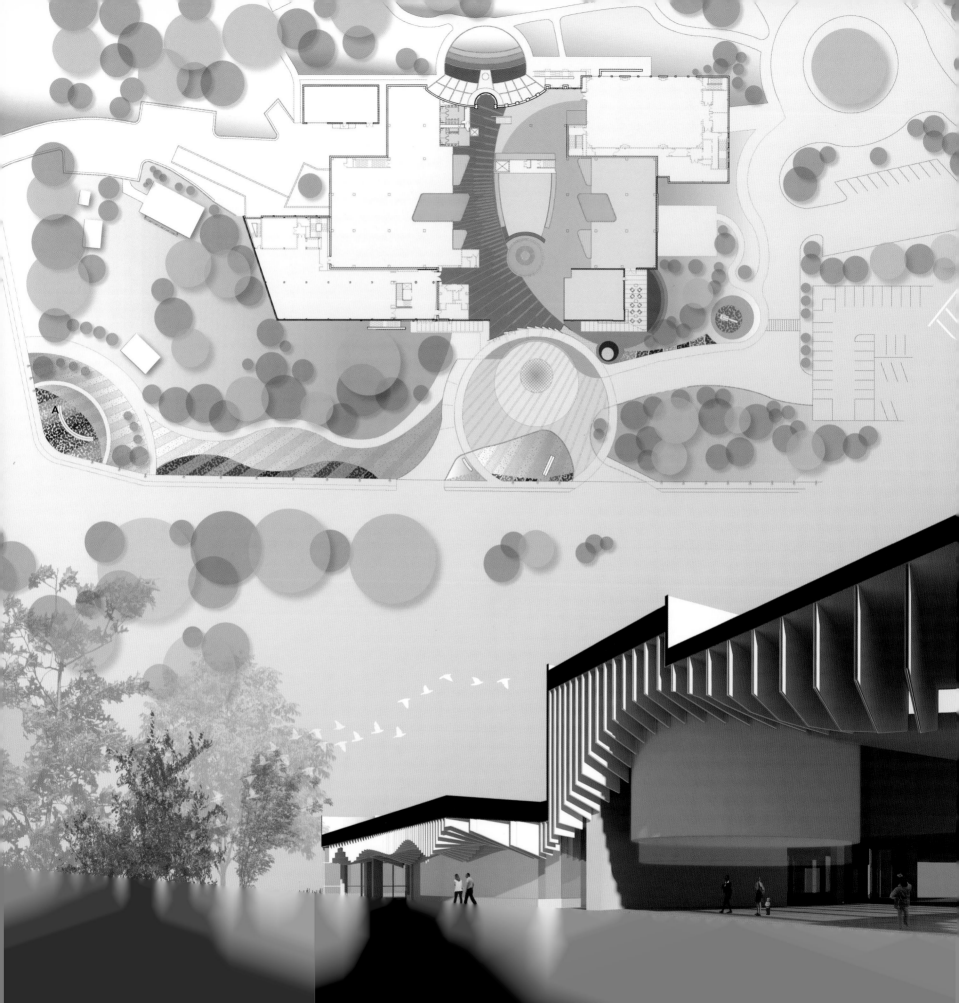

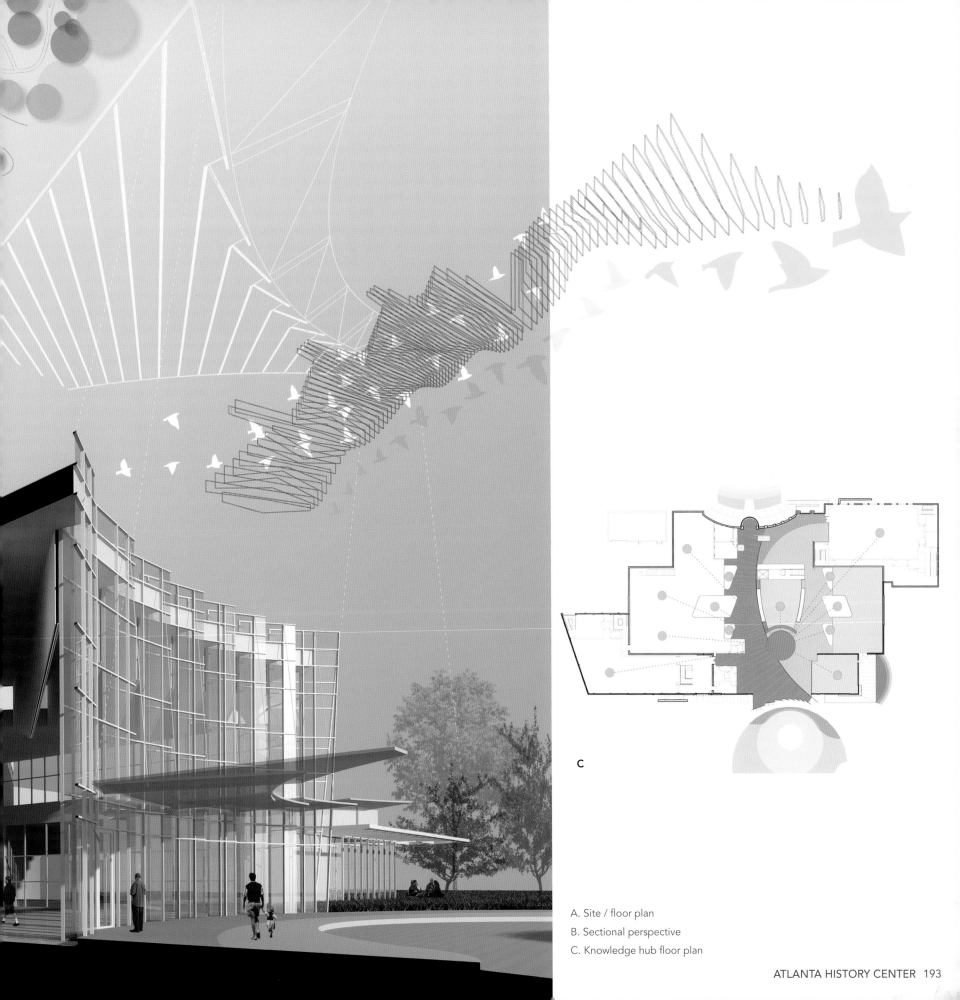

A. Site / floor plan

B. Sectional perspective

C. Knowledge hub floor plan

C

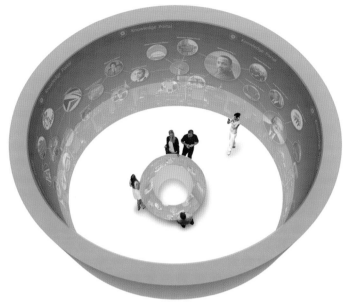

D

A. Hall of enlightment

B. Classroom

C. Main lobby café and museum store

D. Knowledge hub

GEORGIA HIGHLANDS COLLEGE
STUDENT ACADEMIC CENTER
Cartersville, Georgia

In an ongoing story many schools would envy, enrollment has greatly expanded at the Cartersville Campus of Georgia Highlands College, a two-year associate degree-granting unit of the University System of Georgia established in 1968, since its first facility opened in 2005. Confronting this growing enrollment, GHC's desire to strengthen STEM-based areas of study, and Cartersville's goal to open on-site chemistry and microbiology laboratories--so students will no longer need to travel to GHC's Floyd Campus--GHC has embarked on the development of a new academic building at Cartersville. The three-story, 67,700-square-foot structure, designed by Stanley Beaman & Sears, will provide such accommodations as a well-equipped lecture hall, state-of-the-art chemistry and microbiology laboratories and computer classrooms. To encourage science students to be stimulated by the arts--and vice versa--there are also art classrooms to "cross pollinate" the disciplines, expanding the building's orientation from STEM to STEAM, or science, technology, engineering, art and mathematics.

The design responds directly to the College's request for efficient, cost-effective facilities to support current degree programs. First, it includes flexible laboratories and associated support spaces, nearly tripling the laboratory space on compass. To maximize efficiency, the building incorporates flexible modules so it can accept a combination of classrooms, laboratories and laboratory support spaces within each structural bay, optimizing the efficiency of structural and environmental systems, and finishes have been selected to be durable, easily maintained and appropriate to the environments where they are used. Finally, the project has remained on budget at all major checkpoints of the design.

But the new facility will do more than add space. As befits the high aspirations of GHC for its five campuses, there is a common student gathering and group education space called "Main Street" within the building's flexible learning environments to help the Cartersville Campus foster a great learning environment. "Main Street" should also strengthen a sense of place on campus by functioning as a connective link to the two other major campus buildings and the community beyond, counteracting the transitory feeling that pervades so many commuter schools.

Main entry

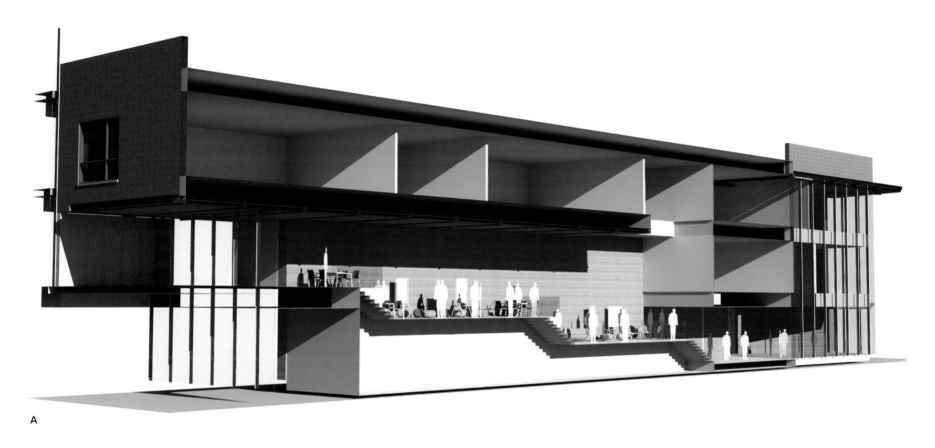

A

B

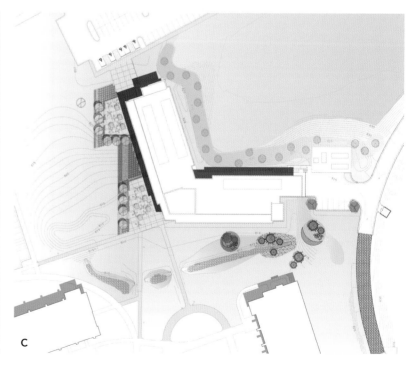

C

A. Sectional model

B. Collaboration space / art wall

C. Site plan

D. Student study rooms

E. Computer model of "main street"

WEST VIRGINIA UNIVERSITY
SCHOOL OF DENTISTRY

As the only dental school in West Virginia, a state that leads the nation in childhood cavities, adult tooth loss, and gum disease, West Virginia University School of Dentistry has played a crucial role in maintaining the state's oral health. Its accomplishments are impressive. More than half of all West Virginia residents admitted to the School of Dentistry remain in state to practice after graduation, and 81 percent of the state's practicing dentists are West Virginia University alumni.

Although the School of Dentistry has thrived with its administrative offices, classrooms, student clinic and research facilities located at the Robert C. Byrd Health Sciences Center, adjacent to Ruby Memorial Hospital on the University's Health Sciences Campus in Morgantown, there is widespread support for a dedicated School of Dentistry Building. The University is currently raising funds for the three-story, 250,000-square-foot structure, which will be contiguous to the Robert C. Byrd Health Sciences Center. Meanwhile, Stanley Beaman & Sears has prepared a concept study for the School of Dentistry.

Stanley Beaman & Sears envisions a V-shaped structure with a spacious entry hall flanked by a large wing, containing classrooms, student clinic and research facilities, and a small wing, housing administrative offices. The exterior's angular, contemporary architecture is clad in glass and a perforated metal screen that is patterned after electronic micrographs of subgingival dental plaque, giving the building a richly textured and futuristic image. Inside, the interiors are bright, spacious and crisply delineated. Coming here, dentistry students should have many reasons to smile.

Main entry

Main entry

Twilight view of exterior

Student lobby / collaboration space

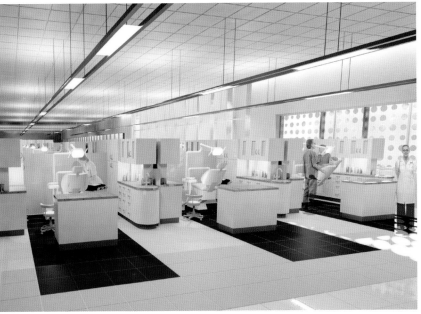

Dental lab

Exterior rendering

CHILDREN'S HOSPITAL OF NEW ORLEANS
New Orleans, Louisiana

New Orleans Children's Hospital, a vital cultural and institutional amenity for families in New Orleans, New Orleans Parish and the State of Louisiana since 1955, has begun an exciting new chapter in its history. Children's 2014 acquisition of the former Marine Hospital, located east of its land-locked Henry Clay Avenue campus, provided the impetus for a long-range master facility plan a year later to establish a modern "academic village" on the Henry Clay Avenue campus, combining a 105,000-square-foot renovation with a 232,000-square-foot expansion.

Now, Children's has embarked on its most ambitious capital improvement initiative ever, assigning Stanley Beaman & Sears to design three key components: Lobby Pavilion, Family Respite Garden and Child Life Department. The multi-phase expansion begins with a new, 600-car parking structure linked to the Hospital by a dedicated bridge terminating at the new Lobby Pavilion, a two-story structure that will serve as the lobby and waiting area for the Ambulatory Care Center. (During construction, the Lobby Pavilion will be the public entry for the entire hospital.) A comfortable, light-filled gathering space for patients, families and visitors, the Lobby Pavilion will incorporate the ACC's registration desk, public waiting area, interactive video wall for entertainment and interactive play, and tribute wall acknowledging benefactors, along with a direct view of the Family Respite Garden.

If the Lobby Pavilion acts as Children's new "front porch," the Family Respite Garden is its new "front yard." Serving as a respite area for parents and visitor, an oasis of refuge for staff, and an anxiety-reducing amenity for patients and families, the Garden will be separated from the adjacent vehicular entry court by landscaped berms. Its saucer magnolias, meandering pathways, banks of indigenous plants, and existing sculptures that have delighted generations of patients will help make the Hospital a more patient-focused institution.

Located strategically on the second floor concourse for easy access from all patient floors, the Child Life Department will address the cultural, spiritual and educational needs of patients and families in a "safe zone" free from stressful medical situations. A teen lounge, toddler/youth playroom, and multi-purpose flex space, designed for staged and special events such as pet therapy, bingo and movie nights, and presentations from the Audubon Zoo, will welcome patients. (An "Exploratorium" with immersive, interactive technologies may also be included.) In short, the Child Life Department will let patients "transform" into children again.

Aerial view of transformation

A. Pavilion and entry court

B. Surgery waiting

C. Main reception / welcome

D. Two-story lobby /
   family waitng

AWARDS

2017	Illumination Awards - Award of Merit Children's Hospital of San Antonio
2017	IIDA Best of the Best Awards - Overall St. Jude Children's Research Hospital Kay Research and Care Center
2017	IIDA Best of the Best Awards - Large Healthcare St. Jude Children's Research Hospital Kay Research and Care Center
2016	The Chicago Athenaeum American Architecture Award OSF Saint Francis Medical Center Children's Hospital of Illinois
2015	Healthcare Environment Award by Contract Magazine - Honorable Mention Angie Fowler Adolescent & Young Adult Cancer Institute
2015	Atlanta Urban Design Commission Gallery 72 – Award of Excellence
2015	Georgia American Institute of Architects Merit Award Nemours Children's Hospital
2015	IIDA Best of the Best Awards Rainbow Babies & Children's Hospital AFAYA – Best of Best in Small Healthcare
2015	IIDA Best of the Best Awards - Healthcare Award of Merit Large Healthcare The Battle Building at the University of Virginia
2014	Richmond American Institute of Architects Honor Award University of Virginia Battle Building
2014	Associated Builders and Contractors FFC Chapter Project of the Year Award Weaver Tower at Baptist Medical Center
2014	Georgia American Institute of Architects Annual Design Awards - Citation Zuckerman Museum of Art Gallery 72
2014	CODA Awards, Institutional: Integration Gallery 72
2013	Interior Design Best of the Year Finalist- Healthcare Nemours Children's Hospital
2013	ENR Southeast - Best in Healthcare Project Nemours Children's Hospital
2013	ENR Southeast - Project of the Year Nemours Children's Hospital
2013	ENR Southeast - Award of Merit for Safety Nemours Children's Hospital
2013	ENR Southeast - Best Project - Award of Merit Weaver Tower at Baptist Medical Center
2013	ABC Central Florida – Best Healthcare project Nemours
2013	ABC Excellence in Construction – Project of the Year Nemours
2013	Healthcare Design Renovation - Best in Category Nadia's Room

2013	Symposium Distinction Awards - User-Centered Award Nemours Children's Hospital
2013	CMAA SAC Project Achievement - New Construction Adamsville Regional Health Center
2013	ASLA Florida Chapter - Award of Excellence Nemours Children's Hospital
2013	ASHRAE Chapter Technology Award – Central Florida Nemours Children's Hospital
2013	AIA - Orlando Design Award of Honor Nemours Children's Hospital
2013	International Design Award - Honorable Mention Nemours Children's Hospital
2013	AIA/AAH Healthcare Design Award Adamsville Regional Health Center
2013	IIDA Best of the Best Awards - Healthcare Top Honor in Healthcare for Nemours Children's Hospital
2013	IIDA Best of the Best Awards - Overall Top Honor Overall for Nemours Children's Hospital
2012	DBIA Southeast Region Design Build Award First Place: Public Sector, Building Under $15 Million Adamsville Regional Health Center
2012	RE-DESIGN Gallery Space Competition Winner
2011	Modern Healthcare Design Award - Unbuilt Category Nemours Children's Hospital
2011	Society of Environmental Graphic Design Merit Award Palmetto Health Children's Hospital
2011	AIGA Atlanta SEED Awards, Professional Print Design Excellence Award winner for the Identity System for Stanley Beaman & Sears
2010	Bentley Systems Be-Inspired Awards Advancing Interoperability Award - Nemours Foundation
2010	ASID Design Excellence Award - Healthcare Kennedy Krieger Institute - Gold Piedmont Spine Center - Silver
2010	IIDA Best of the Best Awards - Healthcare Top Honor in Healthcare for Kennedy Krieger Institute
2009	Contract Design Magazine Healthcare Environment - Honorable Mention Kennedy Krieger Institute
2009	Modern Healthcare/American Institute of Architects Design Award - Honorable Mention - Kennedy Krieger Institute
2009	IIDA Best of the Best Awards - Healthcare Top Honor in Healthcare for Palmetto Health Children's Hospital

2008   Interiors Awards in Large Healthcare by Contract Design Magazine
        Citation - Children's Healthcare of Atlanta

2008   IIDA Best of the Best Awards - Healthcare
        Best of the Best Overall Award - Children's Healthcare of Atlanta
        Top Honor in Healthcare for Children's Healthcare of Atlanta

2007   Georgia American Institute of Architects Design Citation
        Children's Healthcare of Atlanta - Interiors

2007   ASID Georgia Chapter Design of Excellence Awards - Healthcare
        Gold Award - Children's Healthcare of Atlanta - Scottish Rite
        for Product/Custom Design
        Gold Award - Piedmont Physicians Group at Atlantic Station
        Silver Award - Reuter Children's Outpatient Center

2007   IIDA Best of the Best Awards - Healthcare
        Top Honor - Cardiovascular Group Medical Office Building

2007   Healthcare Environment Award by Contract Magazine
        Honorable Mention Children's Healthcare of Atlanta

2006   Modern Healthcare/American Institute of Architects
        Design Award - Honorable Mention - Reuter Outpatient Center

2006   The Center for Health Design Annual Healthcare Environment Award
        Citation - The University of Chicago Hospitals

2006   The Center for Health Design Annual Healthcare Environment Award
        Citation - Cardiovascular Group Medical Office Building

2006   ASID Georgia Chapter Design of Excellence - Healthcare
        Gold Award - Cardiovascular Group Medical Office Building

2006   Southeast Construction Award of Merit
        Cardiovascular Group Medical Office Building

2005   Georgia American Institute of Architects Design Citation
        The Radiology Complex & Women's Imaging Center

2005   American School & University Architectural Competition
        Citation - Comer Children's Hospital at the University of Chicago

2005   American School & University Educational Interiors Showcase
        Gold Citation - Winship Cancer Research Institute

2005   ASID Georgia Chapter Design of Excellence - Healthcare
        Silver Award - Radiology Complex & Women's Imaging Center
        Bronze Award - Winship Cancer Institute

2005   The Center for Health Design Annual Healthcare Environment Award
        Honorable Mention - Winship Cancer Institute

2002   The Center for Health Design Annual Healthcare Environment Award
        Honorable Mention - North Oaks Medical Center

2001   American School & University Design Competition
        Outstanding Building Category - Georgia Pacific Corp Child Development Center

2000   Silver Medal Award/American Institute of Architects - Atlanta
        Outstanding Performance in Architecture- Stanley Beaman & Sears, Inc.

2000   Modern Healthcare/American Institute of Architects
        Design Award - top design award
        for the Medical College of Georgia Children's Medical Center

2000   South Atlantic Regional Conference Merit Award for Interiors
        for the Medical College of Georgia Children's Medical Center

1999   Georgia American Institute of Architects Merit Award
        Interactive Planet

1999   Metal Construction Association Scholarship Award
        for the Medical College of Georgia Children's Medical Center

1999   Metal Construction Association President's Award
        for the Medical College of Georgia Children's Medical Center

1998   The National Symposium on Healthcare Design
        The 10th Annual Healthcare Environment Award
        AFLAC Cancer Center at Children's Healthcare of Atlanta

1998   Modern Healthcare/American Institute of Architects
        Design Award - top design award
        AFLAC Cancer Center at Children's Healthcare of Atlanta

1998   Sixth Annual International Interior Design Acclaim Awards/Los Angeles
        Acclaim First Place Award for custom upholstery design - Deepa Textiles
        Honorable Mention for custom cubicle curtain design - Deepa Textiles
        for the Medical College of Georgia Children's Medical Center

1997   Modern Healthcare/American Institute of Architects
        Design Award- top design award in "unbuilt" category
        for the Medical College of Georgia Children's Medical Center

1996   Georgia American Institute of Architects Honor Award for Excellence in Architecture
        H. J. C. Bowden Multi-purpose Center for Seniors

1996   Modern Healthcare/American Institute of Architects
        Design Citation - H.J.C. Bowden Multi-purpose Center for Seniors

1996   South Atlantic Region American Institute of Architects Honor Award
        H. J. C. Bowden Multi-purpose Center for Seniors

1995   Georgia American Institute of Architects Honor Award for Excellence in Architecture
        Lawrenceville Senior Center

1993   Modern Healthcare/American Institute of Architects
        Design Award - Lawrenceville Senior Center

1993   The National Symposium on Healthcare Design
        The 5th Annual Healthcare Environment Award
        Cardiac Intensive Care Unit at the Children's Healthcare of Atlanta

PUBLICATIONS

2017	Healthcare Design - Cover Halo Effect: the Children's Hospital of San Antonio
2016	New American Architecture - Global Design + Urbanism XVI OSF Saint Francis Medical Center Children's Hospital of Illinois
2016	CODA Magazine: Interactive Art UVA Story Telling Walls
2016	Design Equilibrium, 2016 October Tour: Zuckerman Museum of Art
2015	Architectural Products, November 2015 Museum Piece
2015	Radius Track, November 2015 Framing a Design Inspired By The Spirit of the River
2015	Health Facilities Management, November 2015 Rainbow Babies & Children's Hospital AFAYA
2015	Radius Track, November 2015 Framing a Design Inspired By The Spirit of the River
2015	Curbed Atlanta Unbuilt Projects and the Architects Behind Them
2015	Contract Magazine, October 2015 Rainbow Babies & Children's Hospital AFAYA
2015	The Advisory Board Architectural Design Showcase: September 2015
2015	Design Solutions. Summer 2015 For the Kids. University of Virginia's new medical building houses 36 children's outpatient clinics.
2015	A Healing Journey Supported by Corian (YouTube), July 2015 Rainbow Babies & Children's Hospital AFAYA
2015	Sustainable Architecture Vol.3 Medical+Public+Residential Nemours Children's Hospital and Adamsville Regional Health Center
2015	Healthcare Design Magazine May 2015 Rainbow Babies & Children's Hospital AFAYA
2015	Curbed Atlanta What Should Atlanta Show Off to Architectural World?
2015	Medical Construction & Design The Battle Building at UVA Health System Achieves LEED Gold
2015	Curbed Atlanta The Biggest Development Debuts of Atlanta's Epic 2014
2014	ArtsAtl.com Years in Review: Organizations on the move, our critics' favorite exhibits
2014	CODAmagazine Magic of Color
2014	Abode Magazine, Charlottesville, VA, October Tell me a Tale: UVA's Battle Building aims for happier endings
2014	Interior Design Magazine, August Zuckerman Museum of Art
2014	Health Facilities Management Healing at play
2014	Burn Away Gallery 72 Opens with Sampling of Atlanta Galleries
2014	Creative Loafing From AJC headquarters debut as Gallery 72
2014	Curbed South Downtown Art Resurgence Continues With AJC Building - Downtown Rebirth
2014	Roofing Magazine Adamsville (Front Cover Feature)
2014	HOSPITAL DESIGN + Vol. 2 Tianjin University Press Blanchard Hall, CHOA Egleston Campus, CHOA Scottish Rite, Kennedy Krieger Institute, and Comer Children's Hospital
2014	Atlanta Journal Constitution KSU, Artist in Talks on Controversial Exhibit
2014	Creative Loafing Zuckerman Museum to Open at KSU this Weekend
2014	Arts Atlanta Review: Design of KSU's Zuckerman Museum, Stanley Beaman & Sears, beacon for art
2014	Architectural Record Museum by Atlanta-based Stanley Beaman & Sears Opens at Kennesaw State University
2013	ARCHITECT Magazine Adamsville Regional Health Center Project Detail
2013	gb&d Magazine Adamsville Regional Health and Community Center
2013	HEALTH + DESIGN Nemours Children's Hospital
2013	ArtsAtl.com For innovative Atlanta firm Stanley Beaman & Sears, it isn't architecture without art
2013	Healthcare Design Magazine - March Cover Feature: Nemours Children's Hospital
2013	Health Facilities Management Magazine Designing to Support Infection Control
2013	Healthcare Design Magazine Minding The Myths Of Healthcare Wayfinding
2013	Modern Healthcare Nemours, "Child-friendly, not childish"
2013	AECCafe Adamsville Regional Health Center
2013	Arch Daily Adamsville Regional Health Center
2012	Architect New Health Center will invigorate one of Atlanta's toughest neighborhoods
2012	Creative Loafing Local architects Stanley, Beaman & Sears to redesign old AJC building
2012	Medical Construction & Design New Frontiers - Exploring Options of Prefabrication in Healthcare
2012	Medical Construction & Design Adamsville Regional Health Center Design Embodies Holistic Well-being
2012	Jacksonville Magazines 904 Rising To New Heights- Baptist Health Wolfson Children's Hospital
2012	World Architecture News - January Wings of Change - Atlanta History Center Competition

2011   Health Facility Management - October
Blending Technology & Design - Children's Healthcare of Atlanta

2011   World Architecture News - Wan Awards 2011
West Virginia University

2011   "Lactation Space Design: Supporting Evidence-Based Practice and
the Baby-Friendly Hospital Initiative" - Health Environments Research Design

2011   "The Challenges of Extended Postpartum Recovery for NICU Mothers:
A proposed architectural solution" - AIA Academy Journal

2010   The Year in Infrastructure - Bentley Sustaining Infrastructure
Innovation in Building - Nemours Children's Hospital

2010   Remodel Renovation - Healthcare Design
Medical University of South Carolina Children's Emergency Department

2010   Sign A to Z - Archiworld, Ltd.
Kennedy Krieger Institute
Medical University of South Carolina
Palmetto Health Children's Hospital

2010   Healthcare Design - Showcase
Kennedy Krieger Institute - Urban Oasis

2009   Contract; October
2009 Healthcare Environment Awards

2009   InDesign, ASID Georgia; Spring
"The Changing Face of Healthcare Design" through the eyes of Betsy Beaman, AIA

2008   Interiors & Sources, March, Cover
SBS: Advancing Healthcare by Design - Children's Healthcare of Atlanta

2008   Atlanta Business Chronicle; April - IIDA Awards
Children's Healthcare of Atlanta
Best of the Best
Best of Healthcare

2008   Contract, January
The 29th Annual Interior Awards - Children's Healthcare of Atlanta

2007   College Planning & Management, November - COVER
Facility Focus on University Hospitals - University of Chicago Comer Children's Hospital

2007   Interiors & Sources, July / August - COVER
Piedmont Physicians Group: A Model of Modern Healthcare

2007   Healthcare Design, November
Showcase: Piedmont Physicians Group at Atlantic Station

2007   Healthcare Design, September - Architectural Showcase
OSF/Saint Francis Medical Center and Children's Hospital of Illinois; Peoria, Illinois
Reuter Children's Outpatient Center; Atlanta, Georgia
Piedmont Physician's Group at Atlantic Station; Atlanta, Georgia

2007   Atlanta Business Chronicle; March - ASID Awards
Reuter Children's Outpatient Center
Children's Healthcare of Atlanta - Scottish Rite
Piedmont Physicians Group at Atlantic Station

2006   Healthcare Design, September
Architectural Showcase
The University of Chicago Hospitals
Cardiovascular Group Medical Office Building

2006   Atlanta Business Chronicle; May
Cardiovascular Group Medical Office Building

2006   October, Glass Magazine Project Snapshots
Cardiovascular Group Medical Office Building

2005   Design Cost Data - Green Building Design; November/December - Cover
Winship Cancer Research Institute Emory University

2004   Healthcare Design, September
Architectural Showcase
Winship Cancer Research Institute; Atlanta, Georgia
Radiology Complex & Women's Imaging Center; Tallahassee, Florida
Dugas Building: Faculty Office & Research Laboratory; Augusta, Georgia

2003   Healthcare Design, May
Showcase, "Voyage of Discovery" Brenner Children's Hospital,
Wake Forest University

2002   Architectural Record, July
"Building Types Study" Medical College of Georgia Children's Medical Center

2000   WebMD Health Atlanta; May
"Firm Offers Hospitals a Kid Friendly Makeover"

1999   The Wall Street Journal; June
""Hospital Video Walls Help Healing Process for Kids"

1998   Contract Design Magazine; October
"Four Worlds in One Day"

1998   Modern Healthcare Magazine; October
"1998 Design Awards Competition"

1998   Atlanta Business Chronicle; August
"The Interactive Planet" featuring Stanley Beaman & Sears' design
of this highly successful Internet development company

1998   Atlanta Journal-Constitution, July
"Future arrives Tuesday at Children's Cancer Unit"

1997   Atlanta Journal-Constitution; September
"A Lively Setting"

1997   Stoneworld Magazine; April
"A Granite Emblem of the Past"

1996   Architectural Record Magazine; November
"Opportunities for Architects"

1996   Modern Healthcare Magazine; November
"Cover Story: Design Awards"

1996   Japan's Metropolitan Landscape Magazine, Tostem View; January
"Teaching a Lesson in Architectural Psychology"

1996   Atlanta Journal-Constitution; November - ARTS - Deluxe Design:
"Form, Function in Award-winning Conjunction"

1995   Atlanta Journal-Constitution; September
"Designing Gwinnett"

1995   Featured on the cover of Architecture Magazine; June
"Youthful Spirit"

1995   Child Health Design; Winter/Spring
"Healing Environments in the Age of Technology"

1994   Profiles; March
"Stanley Beaman & Sears, Architecture: Crowding their Canvas"

1994   Profiles; March
"The Lawrenceville Center: About to take Wing"

1993   Modern Healthcare Magazine; November
"Cover Story: Design Awards"

1993   Contract Design Magazine; October
"Putting Families First in Healthcare Design"

GRATITUDE

The award-winning and innovative work of Stanley Beaman & Sears could not have been possible without the many talents and contributions of the following individuals:

Brandon Allen • Scott Allen • Kimberly Bandy • Betsy Beaman • Amanda Bennett • Dawn Mixon Bennett • Lynne Bernhardt • Amy Blanco • Chris Bowles • Paul Bowman • Abby Bristow Chase Brock • Adam Bugele • Jaime Caballero • Clay Cameron • Grant Cameron • Trey Champion III • Helen Chen •Keith Coker • Quintus Colbert • Alfred Collins • Sheila Colon • Leslie Crouch Ali Crownover • Carolyn Daniel • Thomas Danner • Timaio Davis • David Deis • Jennifer Del Rio • Stephen Denton • Brenda Dietz • Simone Dillon • Chris Domin • Kirsty Douglas • Jeannye Dudley Portia Ellis • Lauretta Farmer • Jack Fergusan • Stephen Ferrin • Michael Few • Erli Filto • Stephin Flanagan • Karen Freeman • Godfrey Gaisie • Saray Gill • Margaret Glenn • Donald Glitsis Mariapilar Gonzalez • Jeffrey Goodrich • DeVaughn Grizzle • Douglas Hawthorne• David Heimbuch • Kelly Henry • Tara Rae Hill • Jennifer Hrabovsky • Joi Huang • Sunju Hwang Cynthia Jaggears • Dhruti Jakes • Emily M. Johnson • Emily N. Johnson • Patrick Johnson • Richard Johnston • Paul Jones • Susan Jones • Max Jumper • Rebecca Karlowicz • Fouad Khalil Ellen Kiel • Robin Kirkman • Livia Klein • Janna Kotlyar • Jody Kuehn • Vanessa Lampe-Heimbuch • Kimberly Lane • Silas Laubmann • Joshua LeFrancois • Bill Leggett • Tracy Lemons Meng Li Underwood • Lisa Lin • Sarah Lorenzen • Richard Lyew • Maya Macesich • Marisabel Marratt • Jerome Martin • Randy Maxwell • Gil May • Laura McLeod • Alex Meiser • Jonathan Mickle Regis Mitchom • Yoomi Miyahira • Madison Montgomery • Renita Montgomery • John Moredock • Evan Mott • Anne Mouradian • Nina Murrell-Kisner • Janice Nagy • Scott Newton Mark Novak • Tais Okano • James O'Kelley • Mark Pederson • Mukang Pederson • Elpida Peponi • Brian Peterka • Alex Petersen • Mary Porter • Veronique Pryor • Sangeetha Ramkumar Kathy Rhue • Carrie Rich • Nichole Richard • Michael Rickman • Maita Rivas Shanna Rivers • Kimball Robinson• Brian Rucks • Bianca Scott • Burn Sears • Candace Seda • Pandora Sheridan Ina Sherman • Kaitlin Sinclair • Janelle Slivka • Stephanie Smith • SOBO Network • Kimberly Stanley • Bessie Stephenson • John Stephenson • Allen Stewart • Adam Stillman Zoe Sweeney McMichael • Tammy Thompson • Mekonnen Tibebu • Monica Torres • Marvin Turner • Lisa Vriesema • Chelsea Wagner • Moses Waindi • Rebekah Wallace • Sarah Walter Nelson Weeks • Scott Weinhoff • Ron White • Jennifer Wilkinson • Luke Wilkinson • Sherri Winters • Dena Womak Patterson • Amanda Woosley • Barry Worley • Vivian Chapman

CREDITS

PHOTOGRAPHY CREDITS

©Jonathan Hillyer • Lawrenceville Senior Center • Children's Hospital of Georgia • North Oaks Medical Center • Interactive Planet • University of Chicago Comer Children's Hospital Radiology Associates of Tallahassee • Gwinnett Cardiology Group Medical Office Building • Zuckerman Museum of Art • Adamsville Regional Health Center • Nemours Children's Hospital

©Jim Roof Creative • University of North Georgia: Health and Natural Science Building • Baptist Medical Center • Kennedy Krieger Institute • Roosevelt Warm Springs Institute Blanchard Hall Children's Healthcare of Atlanta • West Virginia University Erma Byrd Biomedical Research Center • Piedmont Physician's Group Children's Hospital of San Antonio Georgia Institute of Technology Clough Undergraduate Learning Center

©Peter Brentlinger • University of Virginia Health System Battle Building

©2014, Hanson PhotoGraphic • Angie Fowler Adolescent & Young Adult Cancer Institute

©Gary Knight • H.J.C. Bowden Senior Multipurpose Facility • Emory University Winship Cancer Institute

©Katy Bricker • Zuckerman Museum of Art • Gallery 72 • Georgia Institute of Technology

©Chris Hamilton • Portrait of Principals

COLLABORATION WITH OTHER FIRMS

- **HKS Architects:** Children's Healthcare of Atlanta
- **HLM Design and Proteus Group:** University of Chicago Comer Children's Hospital
- **NBBJ:** Emory University Winship Cancer Institute; Children's Hospital of Georgia
- **Odell:** University of Virginia Health System Battle Building
- **Perkins+Will:** Nemours Children's Hospital
- **Overland Partners:** Children's Hospital of San Antonio
- **WHR Architects:** Children's Hospital of San Antonio

Published by:
Visual Profile Books, Inc.
389 Fifth Avenue, New York, NY 10016
Phone: 212.279.7000
www.visualprofilebooks.com

Distributed by:
National Book Networks, Inc.
15200 NBN Way, Blue Ridge Summit, PA 17214 Toll Free (U.S.):
800.462.6420
Toll Free Fax (U.S.): 800.338.4550
Email orders or Inquires: customercare@nbnbooks.com

ISBN 13: 978-0-9975489-4-5
ISBN 10: 0-9975489-4-0

Library of Congress Cataloging in Publication Data:
Stanley Beaman & Sears